When Jews and Christians Meet

When Jews and Christians Meet

Edited by

Jakob J. Petuchowski

State University of New York Press

A grant from the Sol and Arlene Bronstein Foundation sponsored the publication of this volume.

Published by
State University of New York Press, Albany

Printed in the United States of America

For information, address State University of New York Press, State University Plaza, Albany, N.Y., 12246

Library of Congress Cataloging-in-Publication Data

When Jews and Christians meet.

Papers presented at the Second Bronstein Colloquium on Judaeo-Christian Studies, sponsored by Hebrew Union College-Jewish Institute of Religion, Cincinnati, Ohio, Mar. 17–19, 1986.

Includes index.

1. Judaism—Relations—Christianity—1945– —Congresses. 2. Christianity and other religions—Judaism—1945– —Congresses. I. Petuchowski, Jakob Josef, 1925– . II. Bronstein Colloquium on Judaeo-Christian Studies (2nd : 1986; Hebrew Union College-Jewish Institute of Religion) III. Hebrew Union College-Jewish Institute of Religion.
BM535.W48 1988 296.3′872 87-9981

ISBN 0-88706-631-3
ISBN 0-88706-633-X (pbk.)

Contents

Foreword

Ever since Pope John XXIII pulled down the curtains that veiled the historic animus between Judaism and Christianity and between Catholicism and Judaism in particular, there has been literally a new world aborning in the field of ecumenical relations. At their very best, ecumenical endeavors, first restricted among the Christian communicants of faith and then expanded to include the Jews as well, have had a telling impact. At their best they have provided a healthy confrontation of differences in ideas and theological commitments and contexts. At less than their best, they have provided a forum among interested parties for the exploration of common ground. In some instances, the motivations for such gatherings were apologetic; for others, they were disguised evangelism. For still yet others, by far the largest number, they reflected a move towards mutual good will and an appreciation for the other as other and for a more profound understanding of the differences which keep Judaism and Christianity as separate faith communities while underscoring the common ground, which has been called the Judaeo-Christian heritage. I believe, despite the doubt cast upon that designation, that such a common heritage exists, particularly as it has developed in the Western world and, most significantly, in the United States.

The Hebrew Union College-Jewish Institute of Religion has for more than a generation been most significantly concerned about promoting the Jewish-Christian dialogue and mutual appreciation that emanates from such an important "ground of meeting." The Sol and Arlene Bronstein Chair, held by my distinguished colleague, Dr. Jakob J. Petuchowski, has been the vehicle for taking our mandate of the mutual exploration of our faiths to yet more significant and telling levels, above merely intellectual confrontations to that of scholarly and learned discourse predicated solely on good will. There have already been two very significant

Bronstein conferences involving some of the most seminal minds in the Christian and Jewish academic worlds. The agenda for these were carefully constructed through mutual deliberations. I am most pleased to have had a generative influence on the creation of both the Bronstein Chair and the conferences and, I hope, the ensuing publications that will emerge from this and future Bronstein colloquia. None of these developments, however, would have come about without the most unusually dedicated and gifted talents of Professor Jakob J. Petuchowski, who, particularly in the last year, despite serious obstacles, brought together a superb scholarly gathering. We are all in his debt, and we pray that God give him continued strength to take this important endeavor to even higher levels of achievement. I want to express on behalf of the Sol and Arlene Bronstein Foundation, of which I am a member, thanks and appreciation to all who have participated in our conferences and have done so much to make them worthwhile.

Alfred Gottschalk
Cincinnati, Ohio

Introduction

Diverse—and, on the whole, unfortunate—have been the circumstances under which Jews and Christians have met during most of the last nineteen hundred years. Whether it was during the relatively short period when Christianity was perceived as a heretical Jewish sect, or whether it was during the much longer period when Jews were sometimes tolerated and more often persecuted as an "infidel" minority in the countries of Christendom, what Jews and Christians had to say to one another can largely be summarized by the phrase "polemics and apologetics." At that, they were usually talking past one another, rather than to one another. That state of affairs changed with the Enlightenment and the Emancipation of the Jews in the West, but only slightly. While there have been, on occasion, friendlier meetings between Jews and Christians since the end of the eighteenth century, the real Christian-Jewish Dialogue was begun only after World War II and, particularly, since the Second Vatican Council's statement on the Church's relations to the Jews, and corresponding declarations by various Protestant bodies.

That Dialogue has by now passed through several different phases. The first phase was the mutual recognition of a common humanity. Christians discovered that Jews did not have horns, and Jews were made aware of the fact that by no means were all Christians either eager to murder Jews or intent upon weaning them away from their ancestral faith. That phase of the Dialogue was an important first step,—a precondition, as it were, instead of an ultimate destination. It did, in fact, lead to a second phase, one in which Jews and Christians became conscious of the fact that they had much in common. In that phase, "good will" was the order of the day. It bred the tendency to stress what the two religions had in common, and to turn a blind eye to the many significant differences. That was the phase during which both Jews and Christians loved to rehearse

Lessing's "Parable of the Three Rings,"—hardly noticing that, in telling that parable, the eighteenth-century German Enlightenment thinker and dramatist could as easily have meant that all religions were as equally false as they were all equally true. After all, religion within that setting only met with approval as long as it met the criteria of a rationally deduced morality and an all-powerful Reason! As Immanuel Kant put it in the title of one of his books: "Religion Within the Limits of Reason Alone." But that stage of the Dialogue, too, has now been transcended. Jews and Christians engaged in the Dialogue today have not only rediscovered the differences between the two religions, they have also learned to take those differences seriously and, what is perhaps even more important, to respect them and even to value them.

It is out of this frame of mind that the chapters of this book have been written—a frame of mind which appreciates the differences and, because of that very appreciation, seeks areas in which Jews and Christians can learn from one another, and goals towards which they can strive together. Thus the first two chapters of this book seek to answer the questions: Where are we going? What purpose do we have in mind when we engage in Judaeo-Christian Studies? What concrete areas of scholarship are awaiting our joint attention? An American rabbi and leading thinker of Conservative Judaism, alas, recently deceased, as well as a Swiss member of a Roman Catholic religious order, who serves as a professor of Judaic Studies, both address themselves to those questions. So also does a Jewish scholar from the State of Israel, who offers his sober assessment of the interfaith situation within the complicated religio-political constellations of his country.

Next, in view of the growing awareness of the fact that the noble and high-minded "ecumenical" deliberations of so many theologians, both Jewish and Christian, so seldom seem to reach the people in the pews, a further topic of this volume is: "From Theory to Practice." Here, a Jewish historian from California and a Protestant clergyman from Switzerland offer information about, and theological insights into, their *practical* work in the field of interfaith endeavors. The Jewish historian, it should be added, is also thoroughly at home in medieval and modern Roman Catholic theology, and the Protestant clergyman is a Hebraist as well as the Editor of the Swiss quarterly, *Judaica.*

For quite some time now, Christian scholars have devoted attention to the scientific study of the Hebrew Bible, and, more recently, some

Jewish scholars have become experts in the field of New Testament scholarship. Of course, modern Jewish and Christian scholars are committed to *objective* scholarship; and perhaps, ideally, no denominational label should nowadays be attached to the scholarly investigation of biblical texts. But both the Jew and the Christian can look back upon some two thousand years of biblical exegesis within pronounced "denominational" frameworks; and those respective exegetical traditions, formative as they have been in the making of even modern Jews and Christians, may have their own value and significance in today's Christian-Jewish Dialogue. That is why, under the heading of "The Joint Study of Scripture," four chapters have here been included,—two in which a Lutheran Bible professor and a Jewish professor of Rabbinics deal with the same passage of the Hebrew Bible, and two in which a Jewish professor of Intertestamental and Early Christian Literature and a Christian professor of the New Testament address themselves to the same New Testament pericopes.

Finally, there is a question which often lurks in the background when Jews and Christians meet to talk about their respective religious traditions, but which, particularly within "organizational" settings with their own vested interests, is hardly ever openly faced, let alone, answered: "Who speaks for whom when Judaism and Christianity meet?" While neither of them claims to provide the ultimate answer, both a Jewish theologian and a Methodist bishop struggle to come to terms with that question in the concluding two chapters of this book.

Part I

Where are We Going?

JACOB B. AGUS

1. *Between Faith and Skepticism"**

Where do we go from here? This question assumes that immense and powerful forces have transformed the Christian-Jewish dialogue. It is as if we of this generation had overcome the demons of dissension which have troubled the minds and beclouded the judgment of previous ecumenical leaders. Have we indeed burst through the gateways of history? Has the messianic age dawned at last? Has history itself come to a standstill?

While we need to take account of the progress that has been made, we have to acknowledge that our task is infinite in depth and scope.

First, we need to recognize the Socratic underpinnings of our world view. Our greatest strength is the willingness to admit our ignorance and, in the depths of our souls, admit that we do not really know the context in which our notions are fixed.

A great Hasidic sage used to say:

> "My brother repeats verbatim whatever I say:
> My son tells me what I ought to say;
> My grandson tells me what I really meant."

The point is, we speak out of our several traditions, but our traditions are themselves set in a variety of contexts of meaning. Consequently, we move within an open society, in which the meanings of the concepts we employ remain undetermined. And as the context of meaning assumes different shapes, the real meanings which we handle in dialogue sessions take on diverse textures of meaning.

* These ideas are developed in greater detail in the author's *The Jewish Quest.* Ktav Publishing House: New York, 1983, pp. 43–61.

Hegel used to say, "An idea is always more than idea." Its real meaning is to be found in the spectrum of concepts ranging between the tendency of self-exaltation and that of self-criticism. Both poles of the spectrum are always in flux.

The Midrash tells us that there are fifty gates of wisdom, of which Moses at Sinai had penetrated forty-nine gates. He had pleaded for the chance to penetrate the fiftieth gate, but the angels set his pleas aside, telling him that if he persisted in his efforts he might find himself back again before Gate One.

Our awareness of the relativity of our knowledge is a pre-condition of our relationship to the words of God. So, the Prophet Hosea speaks of being betrothed unto the Lord in the following order of gradations: "forever," "in justice and in righteousness," "in steadfast love and compassion," and "in faith."

The prophet speaks of a commitment unto eternity, being reinforced through ethical ideals and reaching a climax in faith. But, absolute truth is not listed among these qualities, for it is not humanly attainable.

In the Hebrew Scriptures, as in the writings of the New Testament, we find an awareness of limitation. The Hebrew prophets felt that they were inadequate for the role of a prophet. Moses declined to undertake the mission of a prophet until he was assured that Aaron, the actual shaper of the Golden Calf, would serve as his spokesman.

The prophets as a class of persons mediating between mankind and God, did not stand alone. Beside the prophets, there functioned the priests and sages (Jeremiah 18:18) as agents of the ancient traditions and masters of an international, all-human wisdom, respectively.

When a prophet was given a message covered in symbols, he made sure that the public would know his limitations. An angel, or a heavenly being close to God was described as the one who knew the message. Moses was the greatest of the prophets precisely because he believed himself to be the humblest of all men.

Not only did the prophets acknowledge their human limitations, but the three classes of "men of God" accorded each other full recognition in divine matters. Prophets, priests, and sages could uphold different principles within the same faith and at the same time.

Consider the following rabbinic text:

> They inquired of *Wisdom,* 'A sinner, what should he do?'
> *Wisdom* replied, Evil pursues sinners.

> The same question was put to *Prophecy.* It replied, 'The sinning soul dies'.
> The *Torah* replied, 'Let the sinner bring a sacrifice and he will be forgiven'.
> God Himself stated, 'Let the sinner repent and he will be forgiven'.
> *Yalqut Shime'oni* to Psalms, No. 702

The reply of God does not contradict any of the other answers, but it points to their essential content.

The introduction of relativism into the psychological structure of faith is opposed by many theologians, but we must remember to distinguish between knowing and believing—believing is both more and less than knowing. To believe in God is to refuse to preempt Him. Absolute truth is not available to us. Nor do we accept Martin Buber's distinction between the Greek type of piety, or *pistis* and the Hebraic expression of trust, *Emunah.* It is in history that contexts arise, and their meanings change imperceptibly.

In ancient times, Christian-Jewish relations took shape within the three categories of time: past, present and future.

Anti-Semitism tainted all three dimensions of history. As the rabbis and theologians looked back into the past, they could sense a gradual upwelling of anti-Semitic pressure.

We can arrange the texts, dealing with the Passion in chronological order and document thereby a gradual shift toward a more antisemitic context. The charge of *deicide* was built up generation after generation and then attributed to the Jewish people, without any distinction. No longer were any holds barred—not those between Pharisees and Sadducees, nor those between Hellenistic Jews and Essenic pietists, nor those between pro-Roman families (Herodian) and the rabbinic teachers.

Christianity and Judaism were divided over the interpretation of the Hebrew Scriptures—the identity of Sarah and Hagar, the Edomites and the Amalekites, the succession of prophets, etc.

At the same time, there were the rebellions against Rome (65–70 CE, 111–115, 131–135) and the cooperation of Jews with the anti-Roman Empire of the Parthians and Persians. The bitter invectives of John Chrysostom were the climax of a growing mass hatred that took centuries to acquire passion, depth, and respectability.

It is interesting to take note of the fact that some rabbis were willing to attend debates between Christians and Jews, while others sought to evade such gatherings.

The second dimension of Christian-Jewish relations arose out of the context of contemporary struggles such as the wars between the Persians and the Romans, beginning with the reign of Constantine the Great. The Christians felt that by converting the Romans, there would emerge a situation which would be in large part the fulfillment of the prophetic vision of a universal state: the union of Israel's prophecy, the culture of Athens, and the military power of Rome. The war between the Persians and the Roman emperor, Heraclius was especially significant in this regard, since the Jews of Palestine participated in the war against Rome.

The emergence of the Arabs on the stage of history and their capture of Jerusalem and other cities of ancient grandeur enlarged the domain of disputation without diminishing either its ardor or its extent. The debate was now tri-lateral. Furthermore, the sense of world history was deepened in the Middle Ages, with a messianic hope lending fresh power and glory to the winners of contemporary contests.

The Age of the Crusades reinvigorated the messianic vision and encouraged the various faith-communities to interpret their respective destinies in terms of the ultimate union of military triumph and the spiritual victory of the one true Church.

It is within this tri-dimensional context of history that the current achievements of ecumenism are to be evaluated.

Returning to the central theme of this paper, we find that progress has not always been made steadily and consistently. Ascents to summits of good relations were not seldom followed by descents to dark discontent.

The humanist attitude was achieved, not by the dominance of a set of principles, but by the tension between diverse affirmations. The myths of the Past were balanced by the visions of the Future and revitalized by the challenges of the Present. The resulting tensions left a vacuum, or a Black Hole of sorts, where the creative forces were sucked in and the anti-religious motifs of Communism and Nazism were able to assert their powers.

As we look into the Past, we find that the formative centuries of Jewish-Christian relations can be viewed in different contexts. An inner transformation is likely to take place whereby the fresh attitudes of faith, hope and love are transformed into mystery, miracle and authority.

This insight of F. Dostoevsky is experienced by a historic faith more than once in the course of its development.

So, Scriptural studies are best pursued in situations wherein the contending, critical views of more than one faith are allowed to balance one another. In our day, new proto-canonical documents, such as those of the Qumran pietists, have been discovered whereby the biblical world can be seen in new perspectives.

As to contemporary issues, the issues of social action are pertinent—how best to feed the hungry, how to structure society to promote the growth of freedom, opportunity and equality, how to overcome obstacles to freedom, and to keep the hindrance of prejudice at low levels.

In addition to interpreting the past and analyzing the ethical imperatives of the present, a fruitful society requires a set of inspiring ideas whereby the ever changing social structures are seen in new perspectives and arranged in new categories. "For man does not live by bread alone." New visions of the ideal future are always in order.

We need, then, to move into the future by learning to work together by re-examining the Past, the Present, and the Future. Then and only then will the immense sacrifices of two World Wars not have been offered in vain. Then and only then will the Future loom ahead in bright colors, in keeping with the collective religious heritage of mankind in general and the Abrahamic faith in particular.

CLEMENS THOMA

2. *Where are We Going?*

Almost everybody in the Jewish-Christian field is asking that question. During the twelfth meeting of the International Catholic-Jewish Liaison Committee, held in Rome on 28–30 October 1985, Johannes Cardinal Willebrands declared: "Let us try to see very clearly where we are going, how we should move to get there, and in which way we can already translate our relationship into concrete forms of collaboration toward all men and women, in a world torn by hate, violence, discrimination and also indifference to the poor, the sick, the elderly and the oppressed."[1] And almost everyone declares that, in answering this question, one has to argue from historical, sociological and theological perspectives. There even are some Jews who represent certain organizations which virtually prohibit discussions with Christians on a theological basis. Yet they advance their theological Jewish-Christian thinking without any hesitation before the Pope, in bulletins or in public lectures.

When so many people ask the same question, yet consistently obtain unsatisfactory answers, then something must be fundamentally very unclear or even wrong. In fact, our question concerns the past, the present and the future. As far as the future is concerned, we have no certain knowledge. Nobody is able to see a clear path. Confined to the realm of experience in past and present, we can only analyze why we slid into dead-end roads, and how, in the future, we might be able to avoid superfluous and pernicious quarrels, wars and other inhuman and senseless bloody and spiritual confrontations.

In this paper I am going to emphasize some critical aspects of the modern manner of tackling Judaeo-Christian problems. I would not dare to utter warnings or to judge venerable institutions and idealistic aims, if I were not sure that I am speaking to a thoughtful and liberal audience. My views are the result of experiences in Judaic studies, in the Jewish-Christian encounter, and in Christian and Jewish religio-political action during the last twenty-five years. I hope that my critical remarks will be helpful in paving the way for a more productive teamwork in the field of Judaeo-Christian studies. But I would not like to be counted among Korah and his followers, about whom Holy Scripture notes: *ki hivdil elohé yisrael etkhem me'adat yisrael,* "The God of Israel separated you from the community of Israel" (Numbers 16:9).

1. Introduction to the Problems

To answer the question "Where are we going?" means to continue the discussion we had taken up here in Cincinnati, in 1983. I met a well-read lady, who commented on the publication, *Defining a Discipline,* which resulted from the 1983 colloquium. The lady said that she was wondering whether anybody would be able to add any further essentials to those contained in *Defining a Discipline.*[2] I was unable to agree with her. Surely, in *Defining a Discipline,* it was argued concisely that there exist many Judaeo-Christian traditions on which we shall have to work, and methodological questions which we shall have to ask. But beyond those facts there are still many uncertainties, tentative procedures and deadlocks, with which we shall have to deal in our studies of Judaeo-Christian traditions. Besides, the Jewish-Christian scenery is always changing. New needs are emerging, and, consequently, new responses are required.

We have to occupy ourselves not only with quite a number of methodological and practical scholarly questions, but also with the political and ideological context of our work. "Where are we going?" is not our only question. Quite a number of related questions arise: Who are we? Who are our allies, and who are our opponents? What presuppositions, ideals, and ideologies are manipulating our work? What are the feasible projects that we are able to undertake?

While searching for an answer to the question "Where are we going?," I believe that we first have to clarify our identity *vis à vis* the intentions of other groups dealing with Jewish-Christian problems. Second, we have to declare openly, since there are both Christians and Jews among us, what presuppositions are directing our work. In other words, we have to think about the ideological basis of our work. Third, we have to answer questions with regard to the principal fields of research with which we have to deal.

2. *Identities and Intentions*

In our time, we can already write a history of modern Jewish-Christian teamwork.[3] That teamwork finds its backing in several national and international Jewish and Christian organizations: the Council of Christians and Jews, Actions against Anti-Semitism, Christian-Jewish workshops, and living room dialogues between Christians and Jews. The most influential roof organizations are the International Council of Christians and Jews (ICCJ) and the International Jewish Committee on Interreligious Consultations (IJCIC). ICCJ is an organizational gathering of a number of National Councils of Christians and Jews. It tries to foster a non-anti-Semitic climate in freedom and mutual responsibility. IJCIC, founded in 1970 after much preparatory work by Dr. Gerhart Riegner (WJC) and others, is a specific representative organization. The chief representatives of the World Jewish Congress, the Synagogue Council of America, the American Jewish Committee, the Israel Jewish Council for Interreligious Consultations, and B'nai B'rith are talking with the Vatican, the Orthodox Churches, the World Council of Churches, the Anglican Communion and the Lutheran Churches. Relations with the Vatican are maintained through the International Catholic-Jewish Liaison Committee, on which both the Roman Catholic Church and the world Jewish community are represented by an equal number of representatives.[4] In short, and stated in a simplified manner, the aims of IJCIC are to urge the Vatican and the ecumenical Christian organizations and gatherings to wrestle together with the meaning of the Holocaust, and about a Jewish land-, state-, and people-theology, and about land-and-people politics.

Those aims and their organizational foundations are both very good and necessary. IJCIC, ICCJ and the respective Christian corporate bodies are ecumenically, not confessionally minded. Nevertheless, and this applies particularly to IJCIC, they occasionally have shown some tendencies towards exclusiveness, therein imitating the traditional Church. They are, for instance, the only corporate person entitled to talk with the

Vatican, the Anglican Communion, etc. Moreover, according to their religio-political position, they consider their task to be, in part, a "political agenda," even if they are officially talking about theological, catechetical or pastoral topics like anti-Semitism, Christian preaching, etc. Many scholars, Jewish and Christian alike, are working deliberately in the wake of such organizations. Others withhold themselves from official influences. There are personal and factual tensions between them.

The second group dealing with the Judaeo-Christian tradition and encounter consists of many noble-minded Jews and Christians with a strong intention and idealism to bridge the gap between Judaism and Christianity, and to fight anti-Semitic tendencies. But many of them know only their own Christian or Jewish tradition. Christians are unable to see the points, the centers of gravity, and the requirements of Jewish research. They have an insufficient knowledge of Jewish history, Jewish languages, and Jewish theology. The same also applies to Jews. It is, for example, very difficult to find a Jewish author who is able to write scientifically about the history and the theology of the *kehillah,* the Jewish religious community, in such a way that Christian scholars, who write about the history of Christian religious communities, can understand the similarities as well as the divergencies between Jewish and Christian communities. That also applies to *Halakhah.* There are esoteric articles in the *Encyclopedia Talmudit* which are incomprehensible to non-halakhists, even if they have quite an adequate knowledge of the language and of rabbinic matters. As a consequence, Christian scholars with insufficient halakhic knowledge can do little more than whitewash the Pharisees, in order to avoid anti-Semitism, and to introduce Judaism to Christians as an exemplary religion and community. This may be all to the good, but it is not the whole truth. In this way, the identity of the Jewish people with their venerable history is sometimes expressed in an unfortunate manner by catchwords, including some with dogmatic Jewish-Christian connotations.[5] There are Christian theologians who are taking part in the Jewish-Christian dialogue, and who endeavor to create a better understanding of the history and theology of Judaism. They do so because they regard it as a Christian obligation in view of the Holocaust. However, those theologians are developing an ideology out of their own pro-Jewishness,—which, in turn, is a further negative influence, because it prevents many of their able colleagues from taking part in the Jewish-Christian dialogue. More and more scholars in Europe are stepping aside when this Christian-Jewish dialogue is under discussion. They argue that this is not a reliable science! This fact strikes me as crucial. While there might be some hidden anti-Semites among them, they also do include some serious and valuable persons. We have to try to give them new opportunities to revise their attitude!

The third group dealing with the history of the Jewish people, its languages, philosophy and esoterics is a scientific authority recognized by all who examine and appreciate Judaeo-Christian traditions. Here we mention the *madda'é ha-yahadut,* the World Union of Jewish Studies. That impressive scientific body carries on the studies of the former *Wissenschaft des Judentums* in the Europe of the nineteenth and the pre-Hitler twentieth centuries. It is not possible for a Jewish-Christian scholar to ignore the *madd'é ha-yahadut.* One has to be a member of the World Union of Jewish Studies. However, the *maad'è ha-yahadut* are not focusing on the actualization of Jewish-Christian traditions for Christians. Scholarship in the field of the Judaeo-Christian tradition is, therefore, merely a tributary river to the mainstream of the World Union of Jewish Studies. That should put every serious Jewish and Christian thinker on the alert.

There are, then, topics belonging to Judaism and Christianity which are not elaborated scientifically by Christian and Jewish scholars on the same level. The most striking example are the parables of the New Testament and of the sages of the Talmud. Of all the topics in the New Testament, the parables of Jesus have undergone the most profound methodological studies. That is not so much the case with the parables of the Rabbis of the Talmudim and Midrashim. This has had consequences. The New Testament exegetes believe that they have reached a high level in comparison with the existing exegesis of rabbinic parables. In fact, they consider the rabbinic parables to be somewhat inferior to the New Testament parables. In their view, the rabbinic parables merely refer to Jewish parochial problems, while parables of Jesus are the best literary revelations of the coming Kingdom of God.[6]

There is, however, also an example to the contrary, in the case of Jewish research in the field of Jewish Liturgy. The late Joseph Heinemann and especially Jakob Petuchowski and their followers have made a very good contribution to scientific research. But almost every Christian Liturgy scholar is bound to admit his insufficient knowledge of Jewish Liturgy. As a consequence, he is not even in the position to reconstruct the beginnings of the Christian Liturgy. But we also cannot bestow unstinted praise on the research in Jewish Liturgy. There is a need for a theology, and not just for a history of Jewish Liturgy. Nowadays the famous question about the particular presence of God in the divine service, which had aroused the attention of Jews in Late Antiquity, is very seldom discussed. One can hardly find any systematic discussion about that subject, while, on the Christian side, the theological discussions are overflowing.

The question now to be answered is how an individual, devoted to the Judaeo-Christian traditions and to the actual needs of the Jewish-Christian encounter, should continue to work. On the one hand, we must develop the ability to tolerate and even to celebrate our different starting points and goals. Nobody can wish to contend for leadership against organizations, hierarchies or working groups. We live, search, and teach in a pluralistic and diverse setting. On the other hand, we must form a kind of *scholarly coalition* against narrow-minded perceptions of the Jewish-Christian situation. We have to practise the *criticism of ideologies* on both sides. It cannot be our aim merely to hail theories, ideologies and machinations. We must not dilute our scientific endeavor with non-scientific ambitions. For example, we must not constantly use the post-Holocaust situation as a prop for denouncing our audience as anti-Semites or as bad Christians. We must not make use of our knowledge of Jewish history, philosophy and theology by way of making propaganda for the government of the State of Israel. Doing so would mean making incompetent value judgments and becoming superficial in our field of scientific endeavor by wasting our energies and abilities. Moreover, there are people in Jewish-Christian relations who are like Michael Kohlhaas in the tragic narrative of Heinrich von Kleist. His two horses were stolen by the servants of the Prince of Saxony, and his legitimate demand for justice was not satisfied. This fact caused Michael Kohlhaas to believe in his right to enforce justice even by committing crimes as a revenge on his part. At the end, he was executed for his crimes, because they were incommensurate acts of revenge for the injustice he had suffered. His claim for justice, in fact, turned into injustice.[7] We, in our scholarship, are aware of many and much more horrible crimes against the Jews, not to mention the Holocaust. But as scholars of the Judaeo-Christian traditions we are not entitled to play the role of absolute judge within human society. To stress the required human attitude, I quote the *Sayings of the Fathers: al tehi dan yeḥidi, she-en dan yeḥidi ella eḥad,* "Never make yourself the only judge, because there is not any 'only judge' except the One (= God)" (*Mishnah Abhoth* 4,8). Our time seems to turn into a time of mutual accusations and slander. It should be neither a Jewish nor a Christian attitude to be absolutist in judging our fellow-creatures. What that means for us is that we must be grateful to those who fight honestly against anti-Semitism in the religious and the political fields,— without our creating new injustices at the same time. We have to recognize our common and our individual merits as well as our insufficiencies. In the first place, we should keep a good look-out by practicing criticism of ideologies.

3. Pre-conditions for a Common Scientific Work

I am a Catholic religious clergyman, and I know many Protestant and Jewish colleagues who are friends of mine. We all try to be honest. But how can all of us really pull the same rope? How can my Jewish colleague be sure that I am not an indirect and secret missionary to the Jews or a supercessionist? and how can I be sure that my Jewish friend does not indirectly and secretly have exclusive, narrow Jewish political and ideological interests in mind? An absolute fairness and clarity must exist between Jewish and Christian scholars. Without it, any coalition would dissolve. We must create ties that bind!

Better and more fruitful than merely combatting Christian supercessionists would be the creation of a religious theory of genuine reconciliation and restitution. In the sacred traditions of Jews and Christians we find the idea that all past traditions and institutions are not dead and lost, but will re-emerge to be re-established, re-instated on a higher level in eschatological times. In the Book of Revelation, written some three decades after the destruction of the Holy Temple and many centuries after the disappearance of the Ark of the Covenant, the hope is expressed that God will restore the Temple and the Ark of the Covenant. Revelation 11:19 reads: "Then God's temple in heaven was laid open, and within the temple was seen the ark of His covenant. . . ." And you will certainly remember the eleventh *berakhah* of the *Shemoneh 'Esreh: hashivah shofetenu kebharishonah weyo'aẓenu kebhateḥillah,* "Restore our judges as at first, and our counsellors as at the beginning." If we assume that some of the holy institutions of God's revelation are definitely and completely lost and gone, that the Hebrew Scriptures and the people of God are *only* preparations for the coming of Christ and the Church, then we are merely Gnostics. The Gnostics were convinced that all materiality and all connection of God with the earth will at some time be destroyed. We Jews and Christians have to stand together in the last battle against the Gnostics with all their contempt for history and materiality. Notwithstanding our differences, we have to try to preserve past traditions, to interpret them, and to make them fruitful for the followers of the diverse traditions. Or, as Rabbi Irving Greenberg remarked: "I hope, in the long run, we shall all learn that God's love is inexhaustible, and capable of repeated acts of choosing."[8] Embedded in this hope, we can live and work in a real unity of mind and goal.

4. Fields of Research

4.1.

Within our common Bible there are, as the French say, *relectures*—re-readings, readings in retrospective, actualizations of older traditions for a later audience. After the biblical era there began the *Auslegungs- und Wirkungsgeschichte,* i.e., Apocrypha, New Testament, Targumim, Midrashim, etc. In view of the necessity to work on both open and hidden Judaeo-Christian traditions, we must be competent to give our new *ḥiddush* to the biblical texts and to their representative translations and interpretations. *Ḥiddush* means a new look for traditions. It is a key word within the rabbinic sabbatical preaching. A homily without a good *ḥiddush* is a bad homily. Every preacher must shed a new light on obsolete meanings, create an actualization for a new time and a new situation, and refurbish forgotten or tedious traditions.[9]

Let me give an example. In the Hebrew Scriptures there are stories and judgments about the heathen magician Balaam. In many parts of the Old and New Testaments, in rabbinic traditions and in later Jewish and Christian exegesis, Balaam is not well liked. He allegedly had seduced Israel to apostasy from God and His demands. According to other sources, he was simply a greedy man. Therefore he was deemed to have been the original heretic, an anti-Jewish worshipper of idols; certainly he has no share in the future world.[10] But in the oldest passages (especially Numbers 23:7–10, 18–24; 24:3–9, 15–24) we find in Balaam a very open, sensitive pagan prophet. He proclaims a remarkable theology of Israel, which, in part, could also be a theology in our time. The Book of Esther refers to this Balaam-theology in 3:8. The scholars of Judaeo-Christian traditions would find a field here for their ecumenically minded historical and theological research.

4.2.

Two further fields for joint study have already been alluded to earlier: (1) Jewish and Christian Liturgy, (2) Jewish—especially rabbinic—and New Testament parables. Our task here is a mediating one: we have to control, improve, revise and balance out the lack of methodological standards on the Christian as well as on the Jewish side. Moreover, we have to make transparent the related (different and common) aspects of the two traditions.

4.3.

Those fields of study, which we have mentioned, and other similar fields demand the creation of a common theological language. What do we, or should we mean when, for instance, we speak of Apocalyptic, Midrash, Jewish and Christian theology, Oral Revelation, Liturgy, Messianic time, the presence of God in the midst of His people, etc.? Together with Jakob Petuchowski, I hope to produce a kind of Judaeo-Christian dictionary, in order to enhance a common Judaeo-Christian language. But the task is greater and more complicated than could be accomplished by a mere dictionary. In my opinion, our generation is not yet able to find this common theological Jewish-Christian language. But we all have to work at it.

4.4.

A further special field of research involves a crucial Jewish-Christian period of time: the time between the emergence of Christianity and the consolidation of rabbinic Judaism (ca. 1–138 CE). We have to emphasize that period especially, because, for Jews and for Christians, that period was a turbulent period, filled with uncertainties about how to formulate faith and life, and how to proceed. Both communities had to defend themselves against Gnosticism. Both movements can be viewed as unconscious partners in defending the Creator and the creation against the

Gnostics, who demonized both. It is strange that Gnosticism is very seldom a subject of common historical and theological Judaeo-Christian reflections. Studies of that kind would shed light on the basic character of Judaism as well as of Christianity. Judaism and Christianity are fundamentally defenders of the good Creator and the good creation, the congeniality and election of all human beings, and the teleology of nature, matter, and cosmos. Especially the time before the assembly of the rabbinic *Sanhedrin* in Usha (Upper Galilee) in 138 CE demonstrates that Judaism and Christianity are fundamentally not contrary to each other. Both were divided in themselves, and attacked by the same enemies.[11] Viewing that time of transition—and today all of us, Jews and Christians, are in a similar situation—we understand that Christianity is not simply a daughter-faith, a derivative of Judaism. I should like to refer here to Michael A. Signer, who, in *Defining a Discipline,* page 77, quotes Morton Smith "as suggesting once in a lecture that we cease viewing the early centuries of Church and Synagogue through the metaphor of root and branch, and begin to see it as a flowerbed." Since Gnosticism exists in various forms even in our days, this issue remains topical.

4.5.

Some further very internal and intimate subjects remain to be discussed. For instance: how God's love for His Jewish people is expressed in Rabbinic literature in polarity with God's love for Christ within Christianity. Christ is seemed in Christian tradition as a personal representative of the Jewish people. But God's intimate love for Christ, to a certain degree, pushes His love for the Christian people into the background. When we want to determine the inner differences and connections between Christianity and Judaism, we must see this characteristic point. Christ, not the Christians, must be named in the first instance vis à vis the Jewish chosen and beloved people.

5. *Final Remarks*

As Christians we are in a very uncomfortable and unsettled situation towards Jews and Judaism, because we produced an anti-Jewish history, and we created an anti-Jewish theology. Up to a certain point, Jews, too, are in an uncomfortable and unsettled situation towards the Christians, because some of their traditions were partially perceived almost dogmatically in an anti-Christian sense. I am not going to quarrel with the rabbinic authorities or with Maimonides, but rather with certain anti-Christian patterns derived from their sayings. Jews and Christians have to discuss the shortcomings and deficiencies in the understanding of Israel and "the peoples of the world," and of Israel and the *yir-é shamayim,* the religious persons and groups outside the Jewish people. Here we are at the core of our common task: to find reasonable grounds for a Judaeo-Christian coalition, based on a singular kinship in spite of all differences and oppositions.

Notes

1. *Christian-Jewish Relations* 18 (1985), 7.

2. Jakob J. Petuchowski, ed., *Defining a Discipline:* The Aims and Objectives of Judaeo-Christian Studies, Cincinnati, 1984.

3. Cf. Hedwig Wahle, "Christlich-Jüdische Zusammenarbeit," *TRE* 8, Berlin, 1981, pp. 64–68.

4. Cf. *Activities of the World Jewish Congress, 1975–1980.* Report to the Seventh Plenary Assembly, ed. by the WJC Office of the Secretary-General. Geneva.

5. For an example of arguing in that way, see Pinchas Lapide and Karl Rahner, *Heil von den Juden? Ein Gespräch,* Mainz, 1983.

6. That tendency is expressed in the very influential work of Paul Fiebig, *Altjüdische Gleichnisse und die Gleichnisse Jesu* Tübingen, 1904.

7. Cf. Horst Sendler, *Michael Kohlhaas Gestern und Heute* Berlin, 1985.

8. Quoted in *Defining a Discipline,* p. 38

9. Cf. Clemens Thoma and Simon Lauer, ed., *Die Gleichnisse der Rabbinen, Erster Teil*: Pesiqta deRav Kahana (PesK), Einleitung, Uebersetzung, Parallelen, Kommentar, Texte (Judaica et Christiana 10.) Bern, 1986

10. Those meanings are represented e.g. in Joshua 13:22, 2 Peter 2:15; Revelation 2:14; *Mishnah Sanhedrin* 10,2. Cf. Peter Schäfer, "Bileam," *TRE* 6, Berlin, 1980, 639f

11. Cf. Johann Maier, *Grundzüge der Geschichte des Judentums in der Antike* Darmstadt, 1981; Peter Schäfer, *Der Bar Kochba-Aufstand, Studien zum zweiten jüdischen Krieg gegen die Römer* Tübingen, 1981. Idem, *Geschichte der Juden Palästinas von Alexander dem Grossen bis zur arabischen Eroberung*

Neukirchen, 1983: Günter Stemberger, *Die römische Herrschaft im Urteil der Juden* Darmstadt, 1983; Henry A. Fischel, *Rabbinic Literature and Greco-Roman Philosophy* Leiden, 1973.

GEOFFREY WIGODER

3. *An Israeli Perspective*

A full picture of Jewish-Christian relations necessitates the consideration of both theology and praxis and their interaction. Thus a knowledge of the preceding Christian theology of the Jews is required in the study of the Holocaust, while a knowledge of the Holocaust is required in the study of subsequent Christian theology and action vis à vis the Jews.

With the recognition of the ultimate inseparability of the ideological and the practical, we can build a global paradigm of Christian-Jewish relations. In the first model, they occur between a Christian majority and a Jewish minority. This is the most familiar form because it is the condition of the most crucial manifestation, and is anchored mainly in a Western context where the Jewish minorities are mostly to be found. One cannot talk of Jewish-Christian relations in the Soviet Union, but there is an exchange in certain Eastern European countries which would fit into this framework. The second model is to be found where Christians live without any Jewish population. Here one thinks principally of the Third World, especially Africa, but also the Christian communities of Asia and the areas of Latin America without a Jewish population. In these regions, the Christians have no direct contact with Jews, and precisely because of this, it may be said that the dissemination of knowledge is of especial importance. Third, we have a Jewish majority and a Christian minority—a situation prevailing solely in the State of Israel and for the first time in the history of the Church (apart from its early decades). Fourth, we should complete our model with a situation of all Jews and no Christians, as encountered in areas of voluntary ghettoization by the extreme Orthodox, which applies however only to a few very limited districts, where the world of dialogue would refer at best to the School of Hillel and the School of Shamai.

My subject is Israel, the experience of the third model, and I will at the outset remind you of a few historical premises.

First, the special status of the land of Israel, or parts of it, in the eyes of the three great monotheistic faiths. Each applies the term "Holy," although the nature of that hallowedness and to what it applies is not identical.

Second, the history of the Christian presence has been characterized by unceasing internal strife, especially over control of the Holy Places. A series of firmans by the Ottoman rulers between the seventeenth and nineteenth centuries determined the rights of these communities in the Holy Places. These have been respected by subsequent rulers,—the British and the Israelis—although tensions at the sites have not disappeared.

Third, the Ottoman Empire also introduced the millet system which granted each religious community autonomy in its own religious affairs, including issues of personal status such as the regulation of marriages and divorces. This system, too, has been preserved by both the British and the Israelis. It excludes, for example, the possibility of marriage in the country between people of different faiths.

Fourth, the sole control of the Jewish religious establishment is in the hands of the Orthodox. Whether this could have been otherwise had Reform Judaism embraced Zionism when the modern movement emerged is a subject for a different discussion, but in any case it would be academic, and the fact is that Orthodoxy created facts on the ground and has strengthened its hold as a result of political developments.

A final historical note: Israel's 1948 Declaration of Independence laid down that the State of Israel will foster the development of the country for the benefit of all its inhabitants and guarantees freedom of religion and conscience and the safeguarding of the Holy Places of all religions. Although the Declaration does not have the force of law, its principles have been consistently upheld in Israel's courts. The state apparatus includes a Ministry of Religions—not religion—with a Christian Department and a Department for Moslem and Druze affairs, alongside the Departments for Jewish affairs. These departments have responsibility for the upkeep of houses of worship of all faiths and the maintenance of the respective religious legal systems inasmuch as Jewish, Christian, Moslem and Druze religious judges and ministers are serving as state functionaries when they act as marriage registrars, etc.

Let us now look at the principal actors in our scenario: the Jews, the Christians, and the Moslems. In each case, we have to take into consideration religious, ethnic and political differentiations involving great internal tensions. I will not go into a detailed analysis of the Jewish community, but just remind you of the groupings. The largest element is the "non-observant" (utilizing for convenience's sake a Western category which is not really applicable in the Israeli context; after all, according to Jewish religious law, the very act of living in the land of Israel is one of the highest forms of observance). Among the "observant" there is a bewildering variety: the small group of extremists around the Naturei Karta who do not even recognize the State of Israel; the ultra-Orthodox groups, Hasidic and Mitnaggedic, who have attained considerable political influence, but are deeply divided among themselves into many factions, including most recently a division between the Ashkenazi elements politically organized under *Agudat Yisrael* and the Sephardim under the new and significant *Shas* party. Then we have what has been called mainstream Orthodoxy, whose political expression is the National Religious Party (*Mafdal*), and which controls the Chief Rabbinate and the religious establishment, but which in recent years has lost much of its clout to the more extreme. Progressive Judaism, whether Conservative or Reform, came late on the scene and remains a minor factor in the total Israeli picture, but not, of course, in world Jewish perspective; and the recently formed Movement for Humanistic Judaism which is too tiny to make any impact.

Let me make a generalization concerning all these groups. The vast majority of Jews in all sectors have no meaningful contact with non-Jews. This is partly attributable to geographical factors; the non-Jews, i.e. the Arabs, live mostly in defined sectors of the country away from Jewish centers of population. Since 1967, the influx of Arab workers from the West Bank and the Gaza Strip has brought greater visibility to the Arabs, but this has generally been on an employer-employee basis with social, cultural and interfaith relations remaining the exception. The average Israeli Jew is left with his stereotypes undisturbed, except perhaps for the secondhand impact of the media.

Although our subject is interfaith relations, it should be noted that in Israel these cannot be confined to what the Western world would call "religious" issues. For both the Jews and Moslems, their religious identity incorporates an ethnic dimension and this holds also for the Christians who are overwhelmingly Arabs and do not regard their Christian identity as something apart. Therefore in our consideration of the subject, the *béndathi* is inseparable from the *bén-'adathi*, i.e., the interfaith cannot be divorced from the intercommunal, especially when we mention practical aspects inextricable from the theological-ideological.

Ideally we in Israel should be striving for a trialogue, but there is little participation by Moslems at the inter*faith* level although they are to be found in certain inter*community* frameworks. In the strictly religious sphere the problems of dialogue with Islam are global. Islam is today increasingly dominated, especially in the Middle East, by the more extreme forms of fundamentalism. In some parts of the world, small efforts at trialogue have been attempted, but these usually presuppose the exclusion of any discussion of Israel. This is obviously a distortion for the Jewish participants, and would not be possible in Israel, where contacts between Jews and Moslems ostensibly on religious subjects immediately spill over to hypercharged political, social, and economic issues. Moreover inside Israel, the Moslems suffer from an absence of religious leadership. Their main authorities in the country left in 1948 for the more hospitable climes of Egypt or Syria, leaving a vacuum at the top which has never been filled. There is a drift away from religion among Moslem youth in Israel, and their intellectuals enter many spheres—politics, education, literature, etc., but not religion.

When we turn to the Christians, we may say that never were so few divided into so many. A few statistics, so that we know what we are talking about: We have in Israel 3.5 million Jews. Half a million Moslems live in the pre-1967 borders, and over a million more in the West Bank and Gaza Strip. The Christians number 120,000 in pre-1967 Israel. Of these, 75,000 are Catholics,—with 40,000 Greek Catholics and 30,000 Latin Catholics. 45,000 belong to the various Orthodox Churches, 5,000 to Monophysite Churches, and another 5,000 are divided among the many Protestant Churches. The Protestants, apart from the Anglicans and Lutherans, consist of tiny groups. Nineteen Protestant churches are organized in the United Christian Council in Israel. However, a Catholic has characterized the proliferation of Protestants in these terms:

The Holy Land has, especially since 1948, found itself invaded by a crowd of Protestant sects, especially American. They are sometimes virulent, having access to large resources and often giving themselves to intemperate proselytizing. They have combined to create in Israel a strong feeling of hostility, also virulent, against the "Mission." Under this term thoughtful and informed people think of the sects, but the masses have used the same designation to speak, with equal reprobation, also of the large and respectable Christian confessions. The number of these groups, their variety, their foreign character, and their resources draw a lot of attention.[1]

The categorization of the Christians is complicated. The obvious division is into the local or "indigenous" Christians and those from abroad. Some of the former claim to trace their ancestry back to very early Christians in the Land. However there have always been Christians coming from elsewhere to seek the origins of their faith. It has been suggested[2] that these can be divided into the Jerome-type and the Helena-type. The Helena-type seek their origins through the Holy Places; the Jerome-type through the Holy Scripture. The former have been the founders and promoters of pilgrimage. The latter have not been involved in local concerns; Jerome's opposition to Christian pilgrimage to the Holy Land was due not only to his conviction that this contradicted the universal vision of Christianity, but also because the constant stream of pilgrims to Bethlehem disturbed his studies.

A Dutch scholar, Simon Schoon, has proposed eight forms of contemporary Christian presence in Israel:

> Arab Christians, by far the largest group;
> Christians of Jewish parentage who may relate to existing churches, such as Hebrew-speaking Catholics or Protestants;
> Christians involved in the care of the Holy Places;
> Christians in monasteries and convents;
> Christians who come to Israel as a declaration of solidarity with the Jewish People;
> Christians in Israel for study and dialogue;
> Christians of certain Protestant groups, generally supported from abroad; and
> Dispensationalist groups believing that biblical prophecies are being fulfilled in the State of Israel, and that the end of days is at hand.[3]

It is important to retain a broad perspective and remember the situation in the Middle East as a whole. The tendency to view Israel in isolation can distort the total picture. For example, the frequently heard statement that the Christians are leaving Israel is usually levelled as an accusation. It can be pointed out that since 1967 the Christian population of the country has grown, a consequence of a high birthrate. But Christians are indeed leaving Israel. So are Jews. For both, economic factors are a frequent cause of emigration. But for Christians there is a wider problem of their increasing marginality in the entire region. In recent decades Christians throughout the entire Middle East have been confronted by the growth in Moslem fundamentalism which has rendered their situation increasingly precarious. The culmination has come in the tragedy of Lebanon, which has impelled Christians in various lands to draw a lesson concerning their future under Moslem domination and to look elsewhere, especially in the Western Hemisphere. Some Christians, especially of the younger generation, have left Jerusalem (under Jordanian rule before 1967, the emigration rate was much higher). It is an understandable manifestation of a desire to live in a part of the world in which Christians constitute a majority. Moreover, in Israel, they are not merely a minority but a minority within a minority, and, as they look to the future, the prospect, within the Arab sector of Israel, points to a decrease in the proportion of Christians and a growth in that of Moslems.

One of the problems of the interreligious dialogue in Israel is the absence of most of those elements whom one would wish to be involved, and this includes the Arab Christians. Their loyalty to their Arab identity precludes under the present conditions any compromise with the State of Israel and with Judaism as committed to the return to Zion. They are even offended by biblical references to "Israel" which they feel can be misinterpreted. Their hierarchy tends to identify with Palentinian nationalism. They feel alienated not only from the Jews but also from Western Christians whom they see as motivated by a Holocaust guilt which is an irrelevant concern for Eastern Christians. They played no role, they say, in the persecution of the Jews and, like other Palestinian Arabs, resent what they regard as the attempt by the West to solve the problems created by the Holocaust—both the practical ones of the survivors and the need to absolve the West's feeling of guilt—at their expense, by designating Israel as a Jewish state. In the words of a Greek Catholic priest, Father Elias Chacour, one of the few local Christians to have been involved in dialogue with Jews:

> Jews and Christians from the West have to accept the premise of being either persecuted or persecutors. To us Oriental Christians this type of problem is alien. We never persecuted the Jews. On the contrary we feel ourselves co-persecuted with the Jews. Western Christians who

> accept the main responsibility for the persecution want us Oriental Christians to identify with them in the process of reparation. But we have been and still are the victims of the politicized and triumphant Western Christian world.... The Western Christians who live in our country and our milieu apparently believe that they have been entrusted to monopolize contacts with the Jews and often claim that the Arab Christians do not know how to deal with the Jews. They have assumed responsibility for speaking in the name of the Christians of Israel without paying attention to what the locally rooted churches think, suffer, or consider fitting for their spiritual health. They think and act as though they understand every detail of our lives—except our language and mentality.[4]

As for the Western Christians, we must remember that they are a tiny and marginal group. Very often their impact is more significant back in their Western churches than on elements of the Israeli population. Where they are pastors to a local flock, they have to walk warily because their congregants view with suspicion or hostility their involvement in dialogue. They do, however, inject perspectives that are potentially stimulative, such as modernity in a world of tradition or contemporary ecumenism in a habitual anti-Jewishness.

Turning more specifically to interfaith relations in Israel we could be overwhelmed by the non-starters. Here we have to take into account the large number of people of all faiths living in Israel, who are still ensconced in the Middle Ages. Their thought categories and way of life are dictated by medieval fundamentalism and obscurantism—and this goes for Moslems, Christians, and for Jews who under the impact of a militant nationalism and Orthodoxy have adopted the triumphalism they were denied through the ages, but which they channelled into messianism.

Dialogue and discourse are up against the whole black area of the closed mind and cannot hope to make an impact on the impenetrable. When my son was small he asked me "Do the Arabs know that God is on our side—or is that a military secret?," and in Israel we have a large variety of conflicting elements, each convinced that God is on his side. I have mentioned the Moslems as absent from the discourse. The Orthodox Churches are encrusted in their Byzantine origins and find no common language with their fellow-Christians, let alone with believers in other faiths. After Pope Paul VI and the Patriarch of Constantinople embraced in Jerusalem in 1964, they agreed to establish a Christian Ecumenical Institute which was duly set up at Tantur, between Jerusalem and Bethlehem. But shortly after its opening, the Orthodox pulled out, unable to integrate on a day-to-day basis with Western Christians. Nor do they play a role in the Christian Ecumenical Fraternity (which I will explain shortly).

The Orthodox position is paralleled by the Greek Catholic, which retains a similar heritage, and it is doubtful at this stage whether any breakthrough can be realistically anticipated. Even to open a dialogue with the Oriental Churches is problematic in view of their historical experience, the continuing political suspicion of their communities, and the vast incompatibility of theological sophistication, including even the use of language.

The third group of non-starters is among the Jews. We have the secular non-involved, who, however, are not unsympathetic, and we have the Orthodox hostile. Although some Orthodox Jews do participate in interfaith activities, they are individuals; the bulk, including the establishment, is wary of dialogue. Inside Israel, their strong political clout makes their opposition formidable. They will, it is true, support religious pluralism (as long as it is not applied within the ranks of Judaism); sometimes this is not so much for its own value as out of expedient consideration for the position of Jews living elsewhere. Even supporters of Meir Kahane, who advocate the removal of non-Jews from the State, often are nationalistically, not religiously, motivated. But the newly-acquired triumphalism with its vindication of messianism has crystallized a mentality of superiority. In the powerlessness of ghettoization the Jew was often removed from the world of reality—and indeed this helped to save him. But to be detached from reality when in a position of power is dangerous in the extreme.

The area of origin of the Jews is also significant. We should remember the differentiation between the Ashkenazim, basically Jews of European origin, and the Sephardim, a term used generically if inaccurately, for Jews from the Moslem lands who now constitute a majority of the population. The experience of the latter was primarily with Islam which condemned them for centuries to live as second-class citizens. But they were remote from Christianity—except for the historical memory among the real Sephardim of the expulsion from Spain in 1492 and for the modern experience in North Africa where the advent of the Christian countries of Europe heralded emancipation for the local Jews, who proceeded to merge into the European Christian civilization rather than the local Islamic culture. Suspicion of Christianity is the heritage of Ashkenazi Jews, and is especially strong among those of Eastern European origin (some of them unaffected in their attitudes even if they have come to Israel after a couple of generations in the United States). Seen historically, the mistrust is understandable. Most traumatic is the suspicion of the Christian desire to convert the Jews. For so many centuries the missionaries—in various guises—were among the most feared and hated figures of Jewish life, and this became deeply embedded in the subconscious, a symbol not easily exorcised or discarded, especially by those living in isolation, in a completely introspective existence detached from external developments.

Moreover, we in Israel are plagued by the cut-throat rivalry among the various Orthodox groups which has led to the victory of extremism and the heresy of moderation. It is the extreme Orthodox who make the running with a succession of "crusades," which guarantees them a high profile, with all that that implies in the world today, and the less extreme Orthodox are left with no alternative but to fall in line. The causes may be Sabbath traffic or entertainment, or it might be excavating or building on alleged ancient cemeteries, or it might be the perils of non-Orthodox Judaism, or it might be the dangers of missionaries. The extreme Orthodox in their cause-of-the-month club often pinpoint Christian targets—not as Christians but as Christianizers—and whihp up a hysteria among their followers which in turn has it effect on others, including those who are looking for political advantage from the support of the Orthodox. In recent years, unfortunately, Sephardi elements have become infected and have learned to emulate Ashkenazi fanaticism in order to harvest political benefits.

Finally, from the other end of the spectrum, comes another group of non-starters in our dialogue, namely Christian evangelicals with an open or hidden missionary intent. There are, of course, many shadings of evangelicals and, among the more liberal, some are committed to dialogue. But for the majority—both in the USA and Israel—the agenda does not include dialogue. Their fundamental faith with its literal acceptance of Scripture points in an unmistakable direction in which compromise is impossible. You may respect and work with peoples of other faiths, but the goal is to bring them to your belief. This may be seen as an immediate or an eschatological objective. Many of the evangelicals who come to Israel are dispensationalists or millenarians who acclaim the Jewish State as heralding the Second Coming. Some are content to wait and pray; others feel that an essential prerequisite is the conversion of the Jews for which they are called to witness.

With all these elements outside the dialogue, who is left to be involved and what are they achieving? The core of the Jewish-Christian dialogue is a small group, reflecting the same asymmetry apparent in similar groups in the Western world. For the Jews, Christianity does not pose a theological problem and the Jewish participants do not have the same level of theological motivation as the Christians involved. For the Christians, their very religion has grown out of Judaism, and indeed depends on it; for the Jews there is no relationship of dependency or causality. The Jews are motivated more by historical and pragmatic considerations, based on the conviction that mutual understanding is the key to coexistence.

The leading participants also reflect an asymmetry. The Christians are largely clergymen of Western origin, the Jews drawn from the academic world. Among the Christians, those involved come almost exclusively from pre-1967 Israel. Those in the West Bank are either not disposed, or, if disposed, are wary not to offend their congregants and neighbors. The hub of the dialogue is Jerusalem, but it has proved very difficult to involve church leaders from the Old City except on superficial levels; there have been some exceptions, notably among Protestant groups and some of the Armenians. The main establishments are not involved: the Chief Rabbis, Patriarchs and Muftis do not meet, and the religious institutions are all inward-directed.

Among Christians in general there is the division between those who deny a theological continuity between the biblical promise and post-New Testament Jewry, and hold that the link between Jews and the Land of Israel has been severed, and those who take Paul's words that God's promises are irrevocable as a basis for the belief in the continuing validity of Jewish self-expression in their land. The latter see in the rebirth of Israel a profound mystery with deep theological meaning. The Christian participants in dialogue are among these, and some have come to Israel to try better to penetrate this mystery, which they see as reaching to the origin of their faith. The Jewish people, despite preconceptions, is very much alive and very much kicking. And as this appears to the believer as the proof of God's faithfulness to His covenant people, the notion of covenant is central. Theology here overlaps with history, and the affirmation of the continuing validity of God's covenant with Israel and of Israel's return as its expression, in today's reality, becomes not only a religious but also a political statement. Many of the evangelicals, as a logical expression of their millenarianism, have thrown their wholehearted support behind the Land of Israel Movement, affirming the restoration of Jews to the whole Land of Promise as a confirmation of their religious beliefs. But even other Christians in dialogue seek insights from Jewish perceptions concerning the integrity of religion, nationhood and land.

It is natural that the dialogue agenda in Israel has different emphases from those elsewhere. Outside Israel, theological issues are prominent, while the practical agenda is headed by issues of anti-Semitism, racism, prejudice and the fight for social justice. Inside Israel, the latter subjects are also on the agenda, although often from a different direction, but there is a strong focus on such subjects as the Jewish link with the land, the Christian link with the land through the life of Jesus, and the Jewish roots of Christianity.

Let me mention briefly some of the achievements of interfaith efforts in Israel. The roof body is the Israel Interfaith Association, with a membership of Jews, Christians, Moslems and Druze, which has branches in a number of towns. Here we can see practical activities reaching many elements of the population, down to grass roots. Its declared aim is the fostering of understanding, tolerance, and brotherhood among the different religions and the defense of their religious rights and freedom. It works in three directions: inside the country; among groups visiting from abroad, including the organization of seminars, for example for Christian clergymen from Africa; and its representatives participate on the international scene in the International Council of Christians and Jews and through its Jewish Council in the International Jewish Committee for Interreligious Cooperation (IJCIC). Projects include Jewish-Arab community centers in towns of mixed population and summer camps for Jewish and Arab youth. To enlarge on one program: the Association, in cooperation with the Ministry of Education, has prepared a curriculum for Jewish-Arab coexistence for use in junior high schools. This complements a similar program prepared under the auspices of the Van Leer Institute in Jerusalem for high schools. The object in both cases is to teach about the other, in order to bring to mutual understanding, in the realization that, in the Israel educational system, Jews and Arabs study separately—which is understandable, as even the language of instruction is different—but it means there are no meeting points. It also points to one of the roots of the general problem, not only the absence of encounter, but of knowledge. Little in general is taught about the other groups, and the knowledge of other religions is minimal. The application of these curricula is encountering obstacles, of which the main one is budgetary, as the program is not high on the Ministry of Education's list of priorities, but schools have adduced other reasons for turning it down: lack of teachers' time to prepare, lack of time in a crowded schedule, and the sensitivity of the subject. It has been suggested that parents and teachers in the Hebrew schools feel threatened by a program which sees Arabs not only as individuals, but as part of a people with its own national interests. Moreover, the religious desk of the Ministry of Education has banned any encounters between Jewish and Arab pupils organized under religious school auspices, claiming that such meetings could be accompanied by the consumption of non-kosher food and could pave the way to associations that would end in intermarriage. Some time ago, when Arab pupils were visiting their Jewish counterparts in the framework of an educational program in Beth Shean, the town rabbi demonstrated in the streets, carrying a Scroll of the Law draped in black, with his followers sounding the *shofar* as a sign of mourning, averring that what was involved was *yehareg welo ya'abhor*—a transgression to which death is preferable. One of the shocks to educators in a recent survey was the realization of the extent of support for the racist policies of Meir Kahane among Jewish schoolchildren; in certain schools he won the endorsement of half the pupils. You will note how easily we have moved from interfaith to broader issues but, as I have indicated, these are inextricable in Israel.

Two Jerusalem bodies are theological workshops whose reputation has spread widely. The Rainbow Group, which has been meeting regularly for over twenty years, consists of an equal number of Christians and Jews (originally seven of each, as the colors of the rainbow, with the further implication of the divine promise represented by the rainbow). The pattern has been reproduced in a number of Rainbow groups in other countries, the English one meeting in the Jerusalem Chamber of Westminster Abbey. The other group is the Ecumenical Theological Research Fraternity, also twenty years old, an ecumenical Christian body whose research concentrates on the study of Judaism and the theological implications of the State of Israel. It publishes the journal, *Immanuel,* which

I commend to your attention, as it brings in English translation from the Hebrew outstanding contributions to religious thought and research in Israel, under five rubrics, each jointly edited by a Christian and Jewish scholar: Hebrew Bible; New Testament and the Judaism of the first centuries; Jewish Thought and Spirituality; Jewish-Christian Relations, past and present; and Contemporary Religious Life and Thought in Israel. I will not list the many other interfaith activities and experiments being conducted in Israel, but will just mention the significance of theological research institutions, especially in Jerusalem, where the scene is enriched by a considerable number of Christians who come for periods of study, especially of Bible and archeology, the Jewish background of the New Testament and early Christianity, and Modern Israel. Among the institutions involved are the Ecumenical Institute for Theological Research at Tantur, the Pontifical Biblical Instiute, which every year brings a class from Rome for six months' study at the Hebrew University, the German students at the Dormition Abbey, the Scandinavian and Third World students at the Swedish Institute, and the American Institute for Holy Land Studies, a Protestant school whose students come mainly from North America.

The theological impact of this dialogue is more meaningful for the Christians than for the Jews. I can quote various Christian testimonies for profound changes wrought by the Israel experience which I do not find among Jews, who welcome the dialogue for its sympathetic insights into Christianity and for the broadening of their perspectives. For a Christian reaction, I refer to the writings of one of the outstanding participants, Father Marcel Dubois, a Dominican who heads the Hebrew University's Philosophy Department, a delightful historical irony, as he likes to reminds us, for a son of the Inquisition, and a vivid expression of the positive side of interfaith activity in Israel.

Dubois has written extensively on the subject, and in one of his articles[5] accounts for Jewish existence with the help of several pairings: Israel-Diaspora, uniqueness-exemplariness, faith-observance, and religion-nation, in which he includes land. Most fundamental is the binomial religion-nation. When an Israeli politican quotes the Bible, he says, he is not giving a sermon, but quoting a national cultural treasure; or when Jews in synagogue proclaim the bond between the people of Israel and Jerusalem, they are not making a political statement—they are praying. The bond between the people and the Land is much deeper and more mysterious than mere political Zionism. He finds that the paradoxical consequence of the election is solitude, which has traditionally evoked hostility and scorn, but which he calls on Christians to understand. The paradox of singularity-universalness which is given with election comes to topical expression in the return to Zion, which presents the challenge of being the program/model of all sanctity. The task of Christians is, through love and prayer, to help Israel play this role. In a moving credo, he has written: "In the destiny of Israel, in that of the people of the Bible and also of the Jew throughout history, we see the exemplary figure of the spiritual destiny of Man and we read the Scriptures in this light. We discover more and more that the inheritance of Israel is one of the elements of the Christian identity. We respect Jewish subjectivity and place ourselves in its angle to understand Israel's actual demeanor and vouchsafe to the Jewish soul to be faithful in its own identity. In this perspective the return to Zion seems to imply a return to God, or, at least, allegiance to a mysterious vocation of which Christians rejoice to be the attentive and exigent witness."

One aspect of living in Israel often stressed by the Christians is their unique situation as a Christian minority within a Jewish majority, a turning of the historical tables with lessons to be drawn for both sides. The Jews can learn from the Christian experience, especially the pitfalls of power, while the Christians have much to learn from the Jews' long minority experience, especially in view of their own increasingly minority position throughout the world. Indeed, as even the aspect of Jewish majority is illusory when the situation is viewed in the wider Middle Eastern context, Professor Shemaryahu Talmon has dubbed interfaith "a partnership of losers." But Talmon, one of the leading Jewish participants, has added that the positive side of the Israel interfaith scene is the proof of the interpenetration of the social, political and theological dimensions. Theology cannot be contemplated only on the abstract, scholarly plane, but must act itself out in the realities of group life and individual life. The new possibilities offer a better understanding of the religion-history-people-land complex which has always typified Judaism and is also found to some degree in certain Eastern churches, notably the Armenian.[6]

Now for some of our specific problems. The very special significance of Jerusalem and the Holy Places means here that we are treading on eggs. Nationalist and religious Jews have recently acted concerning the Temple Mount like bulls in china shops, upsetting sensitivities throughout the Moslem world and in a few minutes offsetting years of patient bridge-building. A statement by the Sephardi Chief Rabbi that he is examining—if only theoretically—the question of building a synagogue on the Temple Mount, which would by religious law have to overtop the mosques, would be charming in its naiveté, if it were not a potential match to a powderkeg. We live in dread of extremist action. And, of course, Jerusalem is equally precious to Christians. The official Israel attitude concerning the Holy Sites has been exemplary. They are guaranteed by law, left alone with a certain de facto autonomy, and protected as far as possible—although it is impossible to provide continual guard for the hundreds of Christian institutions in Jerusalem alone. On occasion hostile or criminal acts have been perpetrated. Throughout its long history, Jerusalem has belied the folk definition of its name as *Ir Shalom,* the City of Peace. Tolerance and interfaith respect have been absent; the best to be hoped for was coexistence. Despite the consideration for all Holy Sites, Christianity as well as Islam found themselves challenged by Jewish rule over Jerusalem. For the local Christians this was not so acute, because the Holy Places have been under alien rule for 1,300 years, with the exception of the Crusader century, and their passing from Moslems to Jews merely perpetuated a regrettable situation. For Protestants, the change was also less crucial, as the Holy Sites lacked theological implications. For Catholics, however, the change was basic. Jews, it had been taught, though not dogmatically enshrined, had been exiled from their land as a result of their rejection of Jesus, and their return without accepting him contradicted these beliefs. The earliest papal reactions to Zionism were hostile. Pope Pius X told Theodor Herzl in 1904: "We cannot give approval to your movement. The Jews have not recognized our Lord, so we cannot recognize the Jewish people. If you come to Palestine and settle your people there, we shall have churches and priests ready to baptize all of you."[7] When the British captured Jerusalem in 1917, the bells of Rome pealed out in joy, with the exception of St. Peter's, partly as a protest that the Holy City had fallen under Protestant rule.[8] When this ended in 1948, the Vatican perceived its opportunity to reestablish some form of control in Jerusalem which it sought by pressing for the city's internationalization. The early years of the State of Israel saw strong tensions with the Holy See over this issue. Then the matter was put on a backburner; but, after 1967, the Vatican began to press for "international guarantees" for the city of Jerusalem. While details of such a scheme remain vague and unformulated, the issue of the Holy Sites remains a potentially disturbing factor, while the Vatican has cited the "non-solution of the Jerusalem problem" as one of its reasons for withholding diplomatic recognition from the State of Israel. The return of Judaism as a living force in history in general, and in the Holy Land and the Holy City in particular, is not easy for many Catholics to digest, demanding as it does profound theological rethinking. A block, conscious or subconscious, concerning Jewish sovereignty over Jerusalem is not surprising, especially as those at the helm today were brought up and educated in pre-Vatican Council, and mostly in pre-Holocaust days.

A further problem has been posed by Prof. Zwi Werblowsky, one of the pioneers of interfaith activities in Israel.[9] Can interreligious relationships prosper when there is no intrareligious openness? (Only the other day, I heard a leading Latin Catholic complain that the Orthodox Patriarch is not the voice of Christianity, but the voice of Hellenism.) Jerusalem especially is a microcosm of the fragmentation of Christianity, where most of the Christians are more interested in the status quo than in religious discourse. In light of its unique combinations of religious and politico-national confrontations, the way from polite, or even cordial, coexistence to genuine dialogue is hazardous. Moreover, as we look to the future in Jerusalem, we must be also aware of the rapid change in the nature of the Jewish population, increasingly dominated by Orthodox elements of the more extreme varieties. The problem of their lack of sensitivity to the religious needs of others can only grow, and Jerusalem could easily become a flashpoint.

I have touched on the question of missionary activity and the disproportionate reaction aroused. Currently this is being especially directed against the Mormons and the establishment of a branch of Brigham Young University on Mount Scopus (and here I must state that I, too, feel that the prominence and delicacy of the site granted for the building displayed a lack of forethought). The Mormons have had students in Jerusalem for approximately twenty years, and have faithfully maintained their undertaking not to attempt to proselytize in Israel. But the issue is not the Mormons per se. It is to be found in the intrareligious Orthodox Jewish scene—the rivalries among the various groups—as well as the tensions between Orthodox and non-Orthodox Jews. It has been suggested[10] that the real target of the Orthodox Jew is not so much Christian or Mormon missions, but the secular Jews who represent the even greater danger of humanist intellectualism. Only by whipping up a fanatical parochialism among their followers, especially in the younger generation, can the Orthodox youth safely be guarded from the temptations of non-extreme Orthodoxy. The immediate quarrel of the Orthodox is not with the Mormons but with the civil authorities, with the Mormons providing the pretext.

It is not that missionary activity is generally approved in Israel society, and indeed any Christian encounters suspicion regarding at least his ultimate motive. I have heard Jews comment that while they can trust their individual Christian friend not to seek to convert them, they remain suspicious of the motivations of his church. For the evangelical Christian the problem is the contradiction of his view of religious identity as voluntaristic and the Jewish concept of a religio-ethnic identity, renunciation of which, in the Israeli atmosphere, is seen as treachery. The effect of the Holocaust is also frequently adduced in this connection with the suggestion of the tastelessness of attempting further to attenuate the numbers of the Jewish people after the Great Catastrophe. Evangelicals tend to interpret opposition to organized missions as enmity towards Christianity. On this issue, differences are to be discerned concerning the nature of religious freedom. For many Jews and Christians, this means not only the protection of minorities against harassment and social and political disabilities, but also the right to be left alone. For the evangelicals, it means that the majority Jewish community must tolerate active missionary endeavors. Jews, for their part, have difficulty in distinguishing between "witness," whose legitimacy can be granted, and "evangelization" which is unacceptable. Freedom of speech has to entail the right to attempt to persuade another person to change his faith. So far, Israel's democracy has stood up well to challenges on this score. In 1977, the ultra-Orthodox tried to railroad an anti-missionary law through the Knesset while the attention of the nation was riveted on the visit of Egyptian President Sadat. But even then they were completely rebuffed in their original intention, and only got support for a bill forbidding the offering of material enticement to induce anyone to change his religion (in any direction)—a reasonable law—and one that has not be invoked to this day.

In fact the number of Jews converting to Christianity in Israel is infinitesimal—during the State's first twenty years, the average was about six a year, and I doubt if the figure is much higher today. Certainly it is far exceeded by the number of Christians converting to Judaism. Traditionally, the main success of Christian missionaries in the Holy Land has been the winning of adherents from other branches of Christianity. Different degrees can be discerned in the Christian attitudes to proselytization. At one end of the spectrum are the high-powered missionaries; the less highly-motivated accept the Christian hope for Jewish conversion, but feel that direct action in the current situation is inappropriate (most Christians in Israel probably fall into this category). The third, and perhaps the smallest, group rejects even the proselytization ideal, and acknowledges the validity of the Jewish way to God. These are the Christians working with Jews in an atmosphere of reconciliation and respect. A pragmatic approach on the issue was advocated by Eugene Carson Blake when he was General Secretary of the World Council of Churches: "Our concern in Israel should be voiced in terms of service rather than mission. Mission, in the sense of Christian witness, is in Israel a very dirty word. It is understood by Jews exclusively in terms of proselytizing."[11]

A Jewish reaction to this has been expressed by Shemaryahu Talmon, "Once the admitted 'permanence' of the others' religion is agreed upon, it is obvious that the aim of dialogue must be to become better informed on each other's tenets and beliefs, and to work out a system of livable coexistence. This admittedly does not exclude the possibility of conversions. Anybody who willingly enters into a dialogue takes the risk of having his ideas influenced. But the dialogue situation imposes on us the obligation to curb any attempts at exploiting the situation of the underprivileged for the furthering of missionary aims."[12]

The international dimensions and implications of our subject call for another lecture, but I would like just to indicate certain aspects. In international interfaith encounters, much attention is paid to the subject of Israel, both because of its importance for the Jewish participants and their self-understanding and because of the difficulties of the Christians to understand and accept. With two groups—Islam and the Evangelicals—the issue is clearcut, the former adopting an attitude of unalloyed hostility, the latter of identification. The friendship of the Evangelicals poses a dilemma, well known to the American Jewish Community: the support for Israel on the one hand, and the theological motivations as well as the reactionary conservatism of the believers on the other. The conflicting pulls of ideology and expediency have been decided in favor of the latter by certain Israelis who would otherwise be horrified by a missionary approach.

For both Catholics and mainline Protestants, Israel poses ideological and pragmatic problems. I have mentioned traditional Catholic attitudes, but would like to refer to three recent statements. One is the Pope's 1984 Easter message with the words: "For the Jewish People who live in the State of Israel and who preserve in that land such precious testimonies to their history and their faith, we must ask for the desired security and due tranquility that is the prerogative of every nation and condition of life and of progress for every society." Seen in perspective, even of the last decade, this seemed to represent a significant step forward. The "Notes" on the teaching of Jews and Judaism issued by the Vatican in 1985 is rather convoluted on the subject of Israel. It speaks of the religious meaning of the Land of Israel to the Jews, but disclaims any religious significance for Christians. (As it affirms the continuing validity of God's covenant with Israel, it is not clear how one aspect—the Divine promise of the Land—becomes detached and annulled. The London *Times* asked in an editorial on the document: "If the concept of the 'Chosen People' is still valid in Catholic teaching, why not also the concept of the 'Promised Land'?"). The document goes on to say that the existence of the State "should be envisaged in reference to the common principles of international law." The implications of this are still being debated, with the more optimistic interpreting this as an indication that traditional theology should not be allowed to impede the relationship between the Catholic Church and the State of Israel. The third and most recent statement was in the Pope's homily of 15 February 1986, in which he said:

> "The definitive word of God of Covenant is the Paschal truth which is destined and offered totally to men. Therein lies the definitive fulfillment of the truth concerning the Land promised Abraham and his descendants. That Land becomes for many generations the fatherland of the People of the Old Covenant.
>
> However, the God of Covenant does not fulfill His promise in any single, terrestrial country, in no temporal habitat. Brothers, 'our country is in heaven' (Philippians 3:20)."

The implication here of discontinuity of the divine promise is compounded by an earlier reference to the Church as the New Israel. There are other disturbing statements in this document which do not bode well for Catholic-Jewish dialogue, in general, and the Israel issue, in particular.

Among mainline Protestants, diversity impedes generalization. Some are enthusiastic supporters of the return to Zion, but there are some who still deny the continued validity of the first covenantal relationship, and, for them, the Jews have no right to be in Israel. On the international level, the dispute is politically-motivated, particularly as a result of the strong identification of the World Council of Churches with Third World causes, strongly embracing the rights of the Palestinians. In addition, the churches in Moslem lands play a strong anti-Israel role in WCC circles, while the Russian church presence only strengthens the endorsement of such views. These viewpoints inevitably have a backlash in Israel, negatively affecting the attitudes of Christians as well as fueling the suspicions of Israelis.

To sum up, the question on our agenda is "Where are we going?" I have indicated problems and opportunities, and the complicated fabric with the theological and the political inextricably intertwined. Even more than in the Christian-Jewish encounter elsewhere, we are weighed down with history. We are faced with unpredictable external imponderables that can basically affect the entire situation, notably actions by zealots on all sides. The Jewish-Christian relationship in the West has achieved a basic stability, but in Israel it remains frail and fragile. I can say, perhaps, where we *should* go, but I cannot see where we *will* go until I see tomorrow's newspaper.

Of course, many of the considerations governing the future of interfaith relations in the West will apply in Israel. For example, voices have been heard lately suggesting that dialogue with the Catholic Church has reached a dead end. Those who are involved and committed feel that, even if certain limits are in sight, a great scope remains to fill in particulars and to deepen the impact of what has been achieved. The grass roots on both sides, certainly in Israel, have not been sufficiently affected by the initiatives at the top, and this indicates the direction in which we should now move. With the Protestant churches, much remains to be accomplished, if only out of their variety, but because of their paucity in Israel, the impact of the dialogue there is more potentially significant in its feedback to the West than in the Holy Land itself. This could apply both to new attitudes to missions and to political issues which today via the Protestants in the region help to poison relations with the World Council of Churches and, through it, to the Protestant world at large. One thing is clear: the dream of certain Christians in the West that the Church or Churches have a mediatory role to play in the Arab-Israel conflict is illusory. Ecclesiastically and politically they are committed parties and cannot set themselves up as disinterested mediators.

The real problem as has been indicated, is the relationship with the mass of the Eastern Christians. This is not the same dialogue as with Western Christians, and has not even got off the ground. A recent article[13] appearing in *Immanuel* by Daniel Rossing, head of the Israel Ministry of Religions' Department of Christian Affairs, does not despair of the possibility of dialogue. He points out that the Eastern Christians are preoccupied with issues that include ethnic and national elements, often based on anti-Jewish theologies and attitudes, which over the past forty years have not only not been affected by the Holocaust, but have been sharpened by the Arab-Jewish conflict in the Middle East. Each side, he says, will have to bear the responsibility for the welfare of the other side. Jews, the majority, must be conscious of the heightened sensitivities, fears and suspicions which history has produced in these communities as minorities in the Middle East over the ages, and now under Jewish rule—fears and suspicions not unlike those embedded in the Jewish psyche. These Christians, in their struggle with the Islamic world, must free themselves of the tendency to make Israel and the Jewish people a scapegoat to appease the Moslem overlords, intent on maintaining their traditional colonial hegemony over the Middle East. Rossing even lays out an agenda for dialogue with issues common to both sides, such as the subject of national particularism. Schoneveld has written of the need for a period of tranquility. "The time may not have come yet for a theological dialogue between Oriental Christians in Israel and Jews. It seems at the present moment much more important for both groups to learn to live together, to communicate with each other on many diffferent levels. In modern Israel, their relationship is still so very new and fresh, yet fraught with many tensions, as well as chances, that a formal dialogue on theological terms still seems premature."[14]

The implementation of such a vision will depend as much on political progress as on new theological vistas. Political peace is a *sine qua non* for theological reconciliation. An Anglican scholar working in Jerusalem, Kenneth Cragg, has put it this way:

> Religions claim to be the custodians of transcedent truth, of the truths which ought by definition to unite and bind in one. Yet religions are the most insistent dividers of mankind and never more so than when they ally and align with the political, ethnic and economic conflicts of mankind. Dialogue as an agent of true reconciliation is often in danger of being recruited as a factor in a pseudo-one. True reconciliation means radical acknowledgment of tragedy, an end of assumed innocence and a deep retrieval of enmity."[15]

What goes by the name of religion has been a major cause of conflict in our region. Can it transform itself at this stage from being an obstacle in the way of peace to an instrument of reconciliation? Schoneveld writes on the basis of his experiences in Israel:

> Are Judaism, Christianity and Islam mutually exclusive religions which are in everlasting strife and competition among themselves? Christianity and Islam both have their theories of substitution and suppression of other religions, albeit in different ways. If this is their last answer, then the future is very black and we have to despair of religion as a contributing factor to peace. We should then wish the process of secularization to continue with greater force, although in view of the diabolical forces unleashed in this century by secular man who does not know of any ultimate accountability, we may doubt that this is the proper answer."[16]

I can bring little cheer. Absence of ultimate accountability is no worse than tribal or factional accountability, which has been the record of the relevant faiths down the ages. Those who identify with the modern theological insights developed in Christianity and Judaism in the West will find little comfort and encouragement in any realistic assessment of the prevailing winds in the Holy Land. But hope must be our guide, inspired by other experiences of solving the seemingly insoluble and reconciling the apparently irreconcilable—even in the world of interreligious relations within our own lifetimes. We must take our motto from Rabbi Tarphon in the *Pirkei Avot* (II, 21): "It is not for you to finish the work but neither are you free to desist from it."

Notes

1. Anton Odeh Issa, *Les Minorités Chrétiennes de Palestine à travers les Siècles* (Jerusalem, 1976), p. 2

2. J. (Coos) Schoneveld in *Christianity in the Holy Land,* D. M. A. Jaeger, ed. (Tantur, Jerusalem, 1981), pp. 277–288

3. *Immanuel* 15 (Winter 82–83), pp. 97–98

4. Elias Chacour in *Face to Face* Vol. 11 (Winter-Spring 1977), pp. 8–10

5. Marcel Dubois in *Immanuel* 7 (Spring 77), pp. 78–91

6. Shemaryahu Talmon in "Interfaith Dialogue," special supplement of *Immanuel* (Autumn 73)

7. *The Complete Diaries of Theodore Herzl,* R. Patai ed. (New York, 1960), IV, 1601 ff.

8. Meir Mendes, *The Vatican and Israel* (Hebrew), (Jerusalem, 1983), p. 36

9. R. J. Zwi Werblowsky in *Face to Face* Vol. 11 (Winter-Spring 1977), pp. 7–8

10. David Krivine in the *Jerusalem Post,* 15 August 1985, p. 8

11. *Church and Society,* July-August, 1972

12. S. Talmon, *loc. cit.*

13. Daniel Rossing in *Immanuel* 19 (Winter 84–85), pp. 87–101

14. J. Schoneveld, *loc. cit.*

15. Kenneth Cragg in *Christianity in the Holy Land* (see note 2), pp. 312–313

16. J. Schoneveld, *loc. cit.*

Part II

From Theory to Practice

MARTIN CUNZ

4. *Pastoral Aspects of the Jewish-Christian Dialogue*

I

The Christian-Jewish dialogue—and on the Christian side also a new Christian theology of Judaism—did not spring from the minds and desks of learned theologians. Nor was it initiated by church administrations. Rather does it owe its beginnings and subsequent expansion, after 1945, to persons who had proved their worth in the course of the preceding dark historical and political events. Naturally, there were forerunners of the dialogue and in the field of Jewish-Christian research. Martin Buber, Franz Rosenzweig, Leo Baeck, Joseph Klausner, Karl Ludwig Schmidt and Leonhard Ragaz should be mentioned in this connection. But the real fathers and mothers of the dialogue are, on the Christian side, simple pastors, members of monastic orders, men and women, soldiers and policemen. It is they who, after 1945, made a dialogue of churches and theologians with representatives of the Jewish people morally possible.

Within my purview, the following names can stand for many: Pater Rufino Niccacci from the monastery of San Damiano in Assisi. Together with monks and nuns of his Order, with bishops, simple citizens and even with German soldiers, he saved hundreds of Jews under the most risky circumstances.[1] Provost Heinrich Grüber in Berlin: At the Hebrew Union College it is not necessary to say a great deal about him. From my own country one should name: Paul Grüninger, police commandant in St. Gallen who, contrary to government orders, kept the borders with Austria open for fleeing Jews and made out faked residence permits for them. Carl Lutz, Swiss consul in Budapest: He could issue more than 50,000 letters of protection for Hungarian Jews and thus save them from destruction.[2] Pastor Paul Vogt and Gertrud Kurz: They set up an effective organization in Switzerland for taking in Jewish refugees. The list could be lengthened with names from all European countries.

They are the saints of the dialogue. It is they who, after 1945, gave Christians the courage and inner strength to fight, within the Church, against the centuries-old "Teaching of Contempt" (Jules Isaac) vis à vis the Jewish people. If, today, in many places, Christians not only give thought to a new theology of Judaism but also live in a new relationship with Jews, then this is the spiritual legacy of people like those mentioned here.

An academic theologian, striving to determine the changed relationship between the Church and Israel also theoretically, becomes aware, through these men and women, within what historical horizons he is laboring. And it is because of such saints and righteous ones that there are concrete reasons why Jews, today, are prepared to enter into dialogue and encounters with Christians. Most of these fathers and mothers of such dialogue have one thing in common: Their theology, or their spiritual background was, in most instances, far from friendly towards Jews. Those who were connected with the Church moved largely within the framework of the inherited thought patterns regarding the Jews. Others had, like their contemporaries, even become infected with nationalist and fascist ideology. They could not be led to think about Jews in a new way—who could have taught them?—but they had received the grace to *act* in the right way at the right time. Indeed, the majority of them did the right thing in practice while flying in the face of a false theory. Reflection about a need for change in the theology and attitude regarding Jews often did not begin until after the fact. Those people, at the risk of their lives, had already acted out existentially what Karl Barth was to formulate as a kind of motto for any future Christian theology of Judaism in his Church Dogmatics in 1959: "The Jewish question is a Christian question and a Church question."[3] Their solidarity with persecuted brothers and sisters of Jesus was stronger than their loyalty to a teaching about Christ which had removed and detached him from the Jewish people. Their conscience was stronger than their fear of sanctions from the ruling powers who inexorably punished all non-Jewish solidarity with Jews.

They are the "seven thousand . . . who have not knelt to Baal and whose mouth has not kissed him."[4]

If, today, I am to speak about the way "From Theory to Practice," i.e., about the implementation of dialogists' insights within the practice of the Churches, I would not wish to do so without remembering the fathers and mothers of the dialogue who preceded us in difficult times—going from practice to theory. Their right action within the context of false and fateful theory continues to lead the way, changing our consciousness and our theology. It is as though the *na'ase venishma'* ("We shall do and we shall understand") of Ex. 24:7 was being divided between two generations: what the fathers and mothers *did* is destined to be *understood* and deepened by us.

The relationship between the practical beginnings of the dialogue and its theoretical reception and continuation strikes me as a model for the relation between Church reality on one side and academic theology and research on the other. Theology and research, as well as Christian-Jewish dialogue, receive their legitimation—in the Christian perspective—from the basis of the Church, and its work is, in the last analysis, also addressed to the same basis of the Church. For the situation is not at all that which theologians work out, for their Churches, the theology which then needs "merely" to be implemented, from its basis into practice. Theology reflects the reality of the basis, its relationship to scripture and to the Tradition of the Fathers. Theology lives as a function of this relationship. However, in Christian tradition, it is man, the prime theologian and prime theoretician, who in *theoria* "sees" God and "imitates" God.[5] *Theologia* is knowledge of God and self-knowledge in action, and then, as a second step, comes thinking about this action. *Theoria* and *theologia* are expected of every Christian. The theologian's and theoretician's work, in a modern sense, is only a variety of that which is every Christian's business. *Theoria* and *theologia* contain the total life of the Church.

And here, in the heart of the Christian and of the Church, the dialogists must posit the Jewish question, if, according to Barth, it is to be a Christian question and a Church question. What the fathers and mothers of the dialogue knew intuitively—to the extent that they were committed Christians—gradually penetrates into the consciousness of the Churches since 1945: The attack against Jews hits Christianity in its centre. Even though the 1965 declaration "Nostra Aetate," issued by the Vatican Council, still speaks of Judaism under the heading of "Relations of the Church to non-Christian religions," today we need to understand Judaism not as one of the non-Christian religions—although Judaism defines itself without reference to Christianity and even against Christianity. For the Churches, the Jewish question is *the* Christian question because it is the Christ question. The "Word," which lives within the innermost essence of God, is become a Jewish man. This is the fundamental and eternal reality of Christian identity. The mystery of the Christian congregation has not only its historical, but also its actual roots in the mystery of the congregation of Israel. Applied to the individual Christian, this means that beginning with his or her baptism, a resurrected Jew lives within, not an abstract Christ principle. Through the Jewishness of Jesus which remains beyond His resurrection, there lives in everyone who is baptized the mystery of Israel: not to take the place of the concretely existing Jewish people, as the theologians of all Churches maintained in their disinheritance theories. The Jewishness of the Word of God in Jesus Christ is part of the "Self-Revelation of the Son of God."[6] The encounter with the Jewish people thus becomes, in our post-Christian age, an unexpected and new, yet ancient encounter with Christ.

These highly theological disquisitions which are still a matter of inner-Christian dispute, are of eminently practical significance for work on the basis of the Churches. They make clear, first of all, what this work *cannot* be about. It cannot be a question of preaching *tolerance* to Christians vis à vis Jews, as if Jews were a group of people whom one must tolerate. If, in the strict sense of the word, there is a question of tolerance at all, then it is, rather, the Jews who had to tolerate and endure Christians for centuries. The Enlightenment concept of Tolerance has failed completely, at the very least in our century. Besides, only those who paid the price of outer and inner adaptation to civil-Christian society could enjoy the tolerance of this society. It was precisely that society which handed power to a fundamentally intolerant ideology and thus buried its apparently only superficial tolerance. This is not to malign tolerance. Tolerance would be a good thing if it were practiced. But the preconditions for this do not exist.

But the practical Christian-Jewish work on the basis of the Churches concerns something deeper. It concerns the realization and truth of the dictum "The Jewish question is a Christian question and therefore a Christ question," and the creation of an awareness of this dictum in a spiritual process. Theologically and spiritually we have to deal with the question whether and how we can achieve a position from which to see the otherness and strangeness of Jesus through the otherness and strangeness of the Jews and thus, finally, not only to sustain the otherness and strangeness of the God of Israel, but to accept it within us. The Jewish question, as a Christ question, becomes a God question for the Christian, and *that* in the sense that we become conscious of God as the Strange and Holy One. Jews and Christians stand and fall with the belief that the God of Israel is not the result of human projection but, on the contrary, that He projects His image into man. Man, as in the image of God, is essentially determined in his strangeness. Man's identity is not his own but belongs to the wholly other God.

This is the core of a self-understanding shared by Jews and Christians, but interpreted in their differing ways. I believe it is the Jews who through their *existence* constantly remind the Christian of this basic datum. Their otherness and strangeness, their faithfulness to the strange and other God is the mirror which they hold before the Christian. The experience of centuries shows that the Churches and Christians have difficulty looking into this mirror. They react with fear and rejection. They prefer smashing this mirror to encountering the strange, Jewish visage of Christ, their master, in their own visage. Herein lies the central problem of Christian relations to the Jewish people. And the practical, Christian-Jewish work has to proceed in the Churches within this context.

II

Let me now give you examples to explain how I try to do this in my framework for the Foundation for Church and Judaism in Switzerland. I want to mention beforehand that insights which I explained in the first part of my lecture arose out of this work. The work is not complete. I offer here snapshots of a process which is in flux.

Because one of my main tasks consists in taking part in the conducting of public worship, I have, since I began my work with the Foundation for Church and Judaism, laid great stress on the preparation of *sermons.* At first, they dealt, above all, with texts from the weekly synagogal pericope. Today I interpret, above all, New Testament texts. Because the subject matter of the Pentateuch is, in its narrative portions, widely known and beloved among many Protestants, the introduction of rabbinic interpretations of those texts before Protestants is gratifying and challenging. Naturally, a sermon cannot inform exhaustively on a given topic, but it can select one aspect and deepen it for the listeners. The *transfer* (not the imitation!) of the Jewish reality of believing and experiencing with the aid of an example is more important for the Christian faith than the transmission of a great deal of information. A further danger for the Christian preacher who transmits Jewish interpretations of biblical texts is that he uses the Jewish traditions as a quarry, as it were, to yield good and unusual examples for something he was going to say anyway. This, however, would be nothing but a well-meaning treatment of Judaism as a mere means. It would differ in purpose, not in method, from earlier negative such treatments of Judaism as a mere means by the Church. The preacher's *posture,* however, vis à vis Jewish tradition has to be a fundamentally different one: first of all, he has to school himself in the *posture of a learner* and must transmit this to his Christian congregation. What he learns from Jews and their tradition should influence what he lives and what he says, but it is not its purpose to legitimize his life style. One of the texts which I interpret again and again in order to make a Christian congregation aware of this posture is Luke 2:41–50 (the story of the 12-year old Jesus in the Temple). Luke describes a situation in the house of study where Jesus appears as pupil. Christian iconography completely turned about the meaning of this text as a result of classical interpretations. It turned Jesus the learner into a teacher of the Sages of Israel who close themselves off against his teaching. However, if one explains the original intent of the text, namely to show the Son of God and the Redeemer of the world as a pupil of the Sages of Israel, then the puzzling utterance of Jesus to his shocked parents—"Did you not know that I must be in my Father's house?" (ἐν τοῖς τοῦ πατρός μου δεῖ εἶναί με)—also becomes apparent. According to the plain meaning this can signify: "Did you not know that I have to be among those (the people, i.e. the Teachers of Israel) who belong to my Father?" The consequences for a renewed Christian understanding of Jesus in his Jewishness in the light of this text can be significant. They go far beyond the fashionable figure of the cliché "the Jew Jesus." This cliché is in danger of becoming a new variant of the search for the "historical Jesus." But it is important to liberate the Jewishness of Jesus out of his historical ghetto and to make him into a present-day figure of Christian belief, possibly in this manner: Jesus, Master and Lord of the Christians is a faithful pupil of the teachers of Israel. It is part of his nature to be among them. This *remains* one of his fundamental traits, even as he conflicts with the teachers, and after his violent death. And because being a Christian means to follow in the footsteps of Christ, and "imitatio Christi," it is necessary to make people in Christian life aware of this forgotten and misunderstood aspect of Jesus—anew, or perhaps for the first time in the history of the Church. Not from a gushy or guilty "love" of Jews, but as *followers of Jesus* do Christians today become, like their Master, pupils of the Masters of Israel.

For these reasons it is important for a theologian actively engaged in Jewish-Christian basis-work in the Churches, to be in living contact with Jewish congregations.

For, what is needed is, of course, not merely a Christian theology about Judaism, even if this is a positive one, but a theology and a spirituality which originates in the source of Judaism and draws from it. All this, it must be understood, not for the purpose of judaizing the Church, but to make it reach its most profound *Christian* essence. Admittedly, this is a paradox, but it is a part of the fundamental problem of Christian identity, as discussed above, an identity which, at its deepest level, is an identity of Strangeness. Its core is always elsewhere: with Israel, with Christ, with the God of Abraham, Isaac, and Jacob.

My own personal experiences in Jewish congregations date back to my student days (1964–1970). I regularly maintained such contacts. Out of them arose not only friendship and trust, but also knowledge about Judaism. They provided me with a basis enabling me to let Christian congregations confront Judaism as it is, not as Christians would like to see it. One of my best experiences is, for me, to be taken seriously by the rabbis, even orthodox rabbis. One who genuinely wishes to learn, experiences trust. In this I see the most valuable investment with which progress can be made in the Christian-Jewish work.

As far as the confrontation and the encounter of Christian congregations with Judaism is concerned, this is very often brought about by meetings with Jews. The Foundation for Church and Judaism, together with a mixed group of Jews and Christians, initiated the creation of a four-part film strip with sound track, entitled: "Jews Live Among Us" (Part I: Every Day. Part II: Sabbath. Part III: Festivals. Part IV: History of the Jews in Switzerland). This presentation is well suited to introduce a meeting of Christians with Jews. Jews who are present contribute information about their way of life and their beliefs. Groups of Christians often attend Sabbath services at synagogues. Here, it is not so much information as the prevailing atmosphere which plays a part. Such impressions are then discussed in subsequent conversations. Occasionally, it is also possible to arrrange for invitations extended by Jewish families to Christian people who can then tell wider church circles about their experiences.

It has been our experience that live encounters with Jews, including sermons and lectures, create differeing reactions among Christians. *Fascination* is a frequent response. How could it be different, if one is confronted with what is yours among strangers, or, differently expressed: with your very own strangeness! The fascination goes hand in hand with a perplexity in the face of the actual practice and faith of the Church and of the individual Christian. This fascination often leads to questions pertaining to the *Christian* tradition. By contrast, some people in the middle and older age groups react allergically, at times, to a meeting with practicing religious Jews. "I am glad I don't have to be Jewish and observe all the minutiae of the Law. After all, Christ has liberated us from those things." This is a typical formulation from such quarters. It indicates how many Christians feel insecure and even attacked by a pronouncedly different way of life—much more than by strange credal elements—a way of life which was never intended for them. Such remarks function as defense and veiling mechanisms regarding one's own not fully experienced Christianity and, beyond that, perhaps regarding one's own not fully experienced life in general. The counter question, how *they,* then, live their lives as Christians, every time causes embarrassment and silence. At this point, intensive work of the pastor and educator should set in. A third group might react with the need to *know* more about the Jews. This group forms the basic component of participants in further informational meetings and sessions of all kinds, ranging from religious to cultural and political topics. Included are, e.g., Intensive Hebrew Weeks for lay people and theologians, conducted each year in conjunction with the Catholic Bible Society of Switzerland. Jewish and Christian teachers give instructions in small groups and, through the language, introduce elementary concepts of Judaism. Every such meeting is devoted to a main topic, e.g. Passover, Prayer, the Sabbath, Shavuot, etc. Large numbers of people always register to participate in these Weeks.

At the moment, the following subjects receive the greatest emphasis in the inner-Christian working out of impressions, reactions and information concerning Judaism:

(1) The meaning of God and experience of prayer;
(2) Christology;
(3) *Torah* and *Halakhah*, also Bible interpretation;
(4) Sabbath and Sunday;
(5) Passover, Holy Communion, Passion and Easter;
(6) The State of Israel and the Palestine question.

Permit me to deal briefly with points 3 and 4. Here, we touch on the question of whether and how we, in the Churches, can again find an approach to the "Law" after a complete crumbling away of the traditions and transmitted customs. Especially in Protestantism, Christ liberates from the Law. The distinction between "fulfilling" (Mat. 5:17) and "liberating" is hardly noticed. Law is synonymous with Death, whereas Christ and spirit stand for Life. That Christ is a concrete Way, analogous to *Halakhah*, and that one of the earliest self-descriptions of the Christian community was "the Way" (Acts, 24:14) are notions far removed from the average Christian perception. But the question begins to loom large and powerfully when posed by an encounter with Judaism. Anxiety and curiosity prompt the question: "What are *we,* then, to do?" and it often hovers in the room without an answer, e.g. with respect to the *Sabbath*. In Christian consciousness, the Sunday question is really a Sabbath question, although certain Sabbath laws, especially the prohibition of work, were transferred to Sunday only at the time of Constantine. These matters proved stronger in practice than the central content of Sunday, namely the resurrection of Christ and the celebration connected with it. A re-introduction of the "sanctification of Sunday," i.e. an observance of a meaningful rest from work in the widest sense would, no doubt, be desirable. But the concrete Sunday framework could, in turn, create an awareness of the meaning of Sunday and awaken a joy in old customs, or stimulate the imagination to celebrate Sunday in a new way. The need to walk with Christ as a concrete way, also within the small scope of the family, is generally felt to be oppressive, in view of the inflation of word and action in the Churches generally. Judaism could impel Christians towards concrete instructions—*mitzvot*—without necessarily imitating the Jewish *mitzvot.* According to A. J. Heschel, a *mitzvah* is "an act which God and man have in common."[7] God enters into our deeds through *mitzvot.* As man fulfills a *mitzvah,* representing the divine, a man is asked "to do more than he understands in order to understand more than he does."[8] "Law" is "a cry for creativity. . . . All observance is training in the art of love."[9] Jewish statements like Heschel's, which manage to elaborate experience with *halakhah* positively, are of great help to Christians to find their way back to Christ as the *Torah* of the Christians. Much work is required to dislodge complexes which, among both Protestant and Catholic Christians, stem from traumatic experiences with the "Law" in their own Church.

III

I was asked to say a few words specifically about my work as editor of the quarterly publication *Judaica.* This journal was founded in 1945 by Pastor Robert Brunner, the head of the then Society of the Friends of Israel, today Foundation for Church and Judaism, in cooperation with Professor W. Eichrodt and Professor G. Schrenk. Others associated with the project were famous theologians like F. Blanke, Emil Brunner, K. L. Schmidt, W. Zimmerli and others. Since then, *Judaica* has appeared regularly. Since 1981, the board of editors comprises Protestants, Catholics and Jews. They decide on an editorial plan. Individual members of the board are each time responsible for the issue, the theme of which they have proposed and prepared. The journal's subtitle, given it by R. Brunner, has remained unchanged: "Contributions to the Understanding of the Jewish Fate in Past and Present." *Judaica* is, so far, the only regularly appearing journal for the study of Judaism and the Christian-Jewish dialogue in the German-speaking area. In 1945, it was still conceived in the spirit of the then prevailing Protestant mission theology.[10] The masthead of Number 1 (1945) carries the significant sentence: "The Society of the Friends of Israel . . . considers it to be its task to show forth, among Christians, God's ways with Israel from the Word of the Bible, and to proclaim, among the Jews, the Gospel of Jesus Christ. The journal *Judaica* is dedicated to those endeavors." This declaration, however, did not prevent the editor from publishing already in the first year an article by the then Rabbi of St. Gallen, Lothar Rothschild, on the subject "The 'Jewish Question' from the Jewish Viewpoint."[11] A concern to bring Judaism as understood by Jews closer to Christians was central and determining for Brunner, in spite of his "classical" theological convictions. In 1945 and the years following, nothing beyond that was expected of theologians, in any Church. The shock over the destruction of the Jews did not directly affect the theological perception of Judaism. This is clearly documented in the early volumes of *Judaica*. But the honest discussion with Judaism and the live encounter with Jews—not with theological phantoms—gradually led to a change in perception and finally to a break with the thought of a "mission to the Jews." Its place has been taken by dialogue and an attitude of listening to Israel.

Return, *teshuvah,* is not a one-time act or a sudden event, but a process. The history of *Judaica* makes that clear. Today, the journal sets in where it is a question of promoting the way of the Churches and of theologians from "Teaching of Contempt" to a posture of respect. Jewish and Christian authors have their say with information, studies and expression of opinions about as many aspects of Jewish life and Jewish-Christian cooperation as possible.

(Translated by Elizabeth Petuchowski)

Notes

1. Cf. A. Ramati, *The Assisi Underground*

2. Cf. *Judiaca,* 1/1985, pp. 5–21

3. Karl Barth, *Kirchliche Dogmatik,* IV, 3, p. 1007

4. I Kings, 19:18

5. Cf. Gregory of Nyssa, Vita Mosis II, 252

6. Barth, *Kirchliche Dogmatik,* IV, 1, p. 178

7. Abraham J. Heschel, *God in Search of Man. A Philosophy of Judaism* (Philadelphia: 1956), p. 287

8. Heschel, *op.cit.*, p. 283

9. Heschel, *op.cit.*, p. 307

10. Mission among the Jews as part of a comprehensive mission of the Church. Cf. the programmatic essay by Brunner in *Judaica* 1, (1945), 296ff.

11. pp. 319–341

MICHAEL A. SIGNER

5. *Communitas et Universitas*: From Theory to Practice in Judaeo-Christian Studies

The academic year of 1984–1985 was rich in interfaith celebrations. The decree of the Second Vatican Council, *Nostra Aetate,* occasioned many gatherings throughout the world. Scholars delivered learned papers at the behest of combined committees of diocesan officials and the American Jewish Committee or the Anti-Defamation League of B'nai B'rith. The papal secretariat in Rome was occupied with major "celebrations" for each world-wide Jewish agency. Many of us here at the Bronstein Colloquium enjoyed meeting old friends and finding new colleagues at these gatherings. We lauded the achievements of Jewish-Christian relations over the past twenty years. We made circumspect, and often direct, criticism of the lack of progress among many in the Christian community. We implicitly affirmed our need for one another and the importance of our work.

I would particularly stress our mutual affirmations. We the speakers, not our polite and sometimes enthusiastic audience, made that affirmation. We needed the support for our work from one another because we knew that our passion is often not shared by the broader Jewish or Christian community. The celebrations of *Nostra Aetate* were not attended by massive audiences. There was not a groundswell from the laity—neither Jewish nor Christian—to have any celebration at all. After our papers were delivered, when we spoke informally with one another or with professional staff or lay leadership who hosted our celebration, we could share our frustration about the lack of broader impact of the growing scholarly consensus about Jewish-Christian relations. In our work as scholars who teach clergy and laity we often feel the Sisyphean dimension of rolling the stone up the hill—only to have it roll down again.

There may be a tendency among Christian and Jewish scholars toward frustration in establishing the newly built bridges between us only with respect to the Christian community. We have failed to root out their anti-Jewish stereotypes which often lead to anti-Semitic attitudes. However, we have been no more successful in diminishing anti-Christian sentiment among Jews.

This negative attitude toward Christianity is clearly demonstrated in an article by Rabbi Barry Cytron. He invited a Lutheran pastor to share in a panel discussion with him at his synagogue. The audience was hostile to both of them. When the Lutheran spoke about the newly emerging scholarly consensus of Christians about Judaism, and the Rabbi confirmed these thoughts, the Jews charged that neither the Jew nor the Christian was representative of his community. The rabbi was chided for being "too kind" to Christians.[1] In an impressionistic reading of the Anglo-Jewish press, one observes a sentiment among Jewish laity—not leadership—that any kind words about Christians or Christianity come only from Jews who have a spoiled Jewish identity or who are assimilationists and sycophants.

The rather grim picture of this abyss between scholarly consensus and lay/pastoral reality is what brings us to discuss the problem, "From Theory to Practice." That I should have been asked to discuss this question is somewhat baffling to me. My first tendency is to paraphrase the prophet Amos and proclaim, "I am not a practitioner of Jewish-Christian relations nor the son of a practitioner of Jewish-Christian relations—but an editor of medieval manuscripts whom Jakob Petuchowski took from his desk." Why me? I do not represent an official organization which has promoted inter-group relations. I do not sit on policy-making bodies or boards which could influence opinions in the larger Jewish community.

To discuss the nexus between theory and practice calls me to reflection and introspection. I am a professor of Jewish History who took his advanced degree at the Pontifical Institute of Medieval Studies in Toronto. Since that time I have been involved with activities in Los Angeles because I responded to Samuel Sandmel's challenge in his moving essay, "Antiquarianism and Contemporaneity: The Relevance of Studies in Religion."

Dr. Sandmel described the tension between being well-versed in one's scholarly field and in being able to mediate between that field and the broader world. One side demands analytic skills, while the other side demands synthetic skills. To be a scholar/antiquarian requires a narrow focus; to be a scholar/teacher demands an openness to the world and to human experience.[2] In discussing the problem posed by Dr. Petuchowski, I am also responding to President Alfred Gottschalk's address on the occasion of *Nostra Aetate* when he wrote, "So much research and debate remains confined to the narrow circle of theological specialists, while pulpit sermons seem to continue in the same manner as ever despite authoritarian (sic) admonitions."[3] President Gottschalk further pointed out the failure to change attitudes of lay people despite the new textbooks which are available. Both Sandmel and Gottschalk speak to me because, although I have no official title, I have worked with training both clergy and laity in Catholic and Jewish communities. My academic specialization in twelfth- and thirteenth-century biblical studies also gives me a sense of perspective on the relationship between theological literature and social reality.[4]

Let me state at the beginning that I do not understand theory and practice as antithetical to one another; nor do I believe that the relationship between them is hierarchical. Theory ought not to be some platonized intellectual abstraction which is then poured forth over an unwashed material reality. Rather, I would describe theory and practice as existing in dialectical tension with one another. Paraphrasing David Tracy, I would claim that there is no *fides quae* without a *fides qua*. Theory ought to begin with a reflection upon reality, and then move to a critique of reality. However, it is equally important that theory not become hypostatized and immune from reality. Theory must constantly be critiqued and measured by reality.[5]

My presentation will move through a three-part process. First, I will describe what I call an ecology of interfaith learning: What environments and publics seem to be involved with transmitting the scholarly consensus?[6] Second, I would speculate on some potential results given the current realities. In this section I will describe some scholarly developments from the Christian perspective, and discern how Jews might react. Finally, in the third section, we will ask about the paths that we might pursue together to move forward in promoting the scholarly consensus. How can we break out of the cycle of "affirmations of unity and harmony" which are followed by sloth. Or, as Bialik put it so poignantly, "The silence returned as it was, the mighty lay dead with no tremor."[7]

A. Toward an Ecology of Interfaith Learning

President Gottschalk's address identified the gap between three distinct groups in the realm of interfaith education: theological specialists, pulpit clergy, and the laity. I would affirm that each group constitutes an important link in the ecology of learning any aspect of contemporary religious life. Most of us would agree that if we were to analyze any problem within a faith community that these groups would be significant parts of the learning process. We would also agree that the statement made by President Gottschalk about the sorry state of communication between these groups about Jewish-Christian relations could apply to almost any theological or pastoral conundrum. It is my impression that theological specialists who are mostly seminary or university faculty are not quoted from the pulpit on most topics. On the other hand, pastors and rabbis are often aghast when they hear their pulpit teachings quoted by the laity. Finally, the members of synagogues and churches rarely reinforce the need for their clergy to deliver themselves of learned discourse. They are often frustrated when they hear something new which challenges their reality. Even when we admit that there are some among the laity who yearn for more substance, there is an impression that these "folks who are hungry" constitute a minority.[8]

An important link in the chain, I think implicit in what President Gottschalk stated, is the role of religious educators. These individuals, sometimes ordained clergy, but often lay people with a particular passion, are charged with the task of providing the socialization and education of the youth within the synagogue or church. One usually associates this group with the "practical," the "immediate" task of providing the basis for members of the community to mature and become responsible participants as adults in the church or synagogue. These educators have their own professional organizations; their own journals and professional literature; and their own set of concerns and priorities. For the most part, within the Jewish and Catholic communities, they are not trained in seminaries. The introduction of religious educators into the ecology is significant, because they bear such responsibility with very little public visibility.

We have, then, the following theoretical structure. Seminary professors (those most often invited to speak at interfaith gatherings) produce new knowledge. They train the pastors and rabbis who are consumers and transmitters of knowledge within the synagogue or church. Religious educators are charged by rabbis and pastors with transmitting knowledge which is distilled into textbooks which are often written neither by seminary professors nor practicing educators.[9] The end of the chain, the consumers, is the lay audience which represents a broad spectrum of educational, economic and social backgrounds. This structure, as I have described it, is a hierarchy. The various groups do not communicate with one another as equals sharing a common task, but as superiors and subordinates—as experts and non-experts.

Over the past fifteen years I have been part of this educational structure at several levels. Let us begin to describe this problematic structure with the seminary or institution of higher education. I believe there is a genuine difference between the course of rabbinic studies and priestly formation programs. At Hebrew Union College we value the academic prowess of our students. The power of their analytic mettle is tested almost on a daily basis, as they are required to decode ancient and medieval texts. Comprehension and analysis would be the categories of the educational taxonomy which could be said to be most highly prized by the majority of our faculty. The ability that a student demonstrates with respect to synthesizing his or her ancient or medieval texts with his or her own experience does not receive overt recognition. One colleague, a visiting professor, once revealed this split between analytic and synthetic abilities when he described that, "My students can tell me what Buber said or what Hermann Cohen said about any topic; they are unable to tell me in a coherent and reasoned argument what *they* have to say." These synthetic and personal moments do have their place in the co-curricular events of life at the College. Many long-lasting personal relationships between faculty and student evolve from advisement of a sermon or a bi-weekly pulpit.

I would contrast this experience with my years at St. John's Seminary which is involved with priestly formation. The seminarian is caught, it seems to me, in a tri-partite web of evaluation in academic formation, field work, and spiritual life. If academic achievement is singularly valued by the Hebrew Union College faculty, then the seminarian at St. John's is stretched by a plurality of valued areas of training. The heavy pastoral emphasis at times diffuses the need to demonstrate traditional academic skills. Yet, when students fail to make academic progress, the faculty and students feel a sense of frustration.

It may be the particular malaise of academic institutions that everyone feels isolated and frustrated. The faculty, producers of new ideas, often feel that their students are unreceptive to any ideas at all. Students, who want to serve a religious community, find their classes to be isolated from any reality of that community. An incident from my class at St. John's may illustrate this problem. I was teaching the book of Isaiah, and when doing my exposition on the Emanuel prophecy (Isaiah 7), I concluded the lecture with the words, "Gentlemen, please understand that the prophet was not referring to the messiah or Jesus." A student responded, "Don't worry about that, Rabbi; they took the three wise men away during the first year of seminary, and it's been all downhill since then." We can all make light of the demythologizing which we do in developing critical consciousness on the part of our students. However, we ought to remember that from the laity our students did come, and it is to the laity that they must return. They often look to their professors for constructive guidance about rebuilding their intellectual and emotional *schemata* for organizing their world-view. We as faculty might listen to them, and respond as one of my students did when I asked him about the Eucharist: "First, we need to give our people a sense of mystery—then we can teach them about the nature of the Eucharist." Before we can ask our students to preach and teach the consensus about interfaith relationships, we need to ask whether or not we want to hear their response to us and our teachings as *they* understand them; and not as we want to be understood.

James A. Sanders has put it another way. Do seminary professors see themselves as responsible to the religious community—to teach and to nurture it? Or, are our fundamental loyalties and efforts put toward our "professional guild"? To what extent has our study of sacred texts been removed to our offices and out of the churches and synagogues?[10] Lou Silberman, in his presidential address to the Society of Biblical Literature, asked how much of the process of discovery and adventure do we share with our students? He chided scholars for delivering themselves of the disembodied results of scholarship, and not presenting the exciting process of developing new knowledge.[11]

Students and faculty in seminaries tend to see knowledge within separate disciplines. Interdisciplinary studies would be the model to nurture the discovery of the consensus of Jewish-Christian scholarship. Yet, our curricula are already strained to the breaking point with the distillation of what each group considers to be the *sine qua non* of education for the rabbinate, pastorate, or priesthood.

It is my impression that faculty and ordained clergy do not see themselves as equal partners in an on-going dialogue. The seminary becomes precisely that—a seed-bed from which our clergy grow. They blossom elsewhere. Therefore, we can well understand the gap between the seminary and the pulpit—between those who teach those who will preach.[12]

Ironically, there is a similar gap between those who preach and those who teach within the churches and synangogues. The seminary experience of the rabbi, priest, or minister is repeated in the congregation. Here, the religious educators, those who work in the religious school, C.C.D., or Hebrew school do not engage in dialogue with their rabbi, priest, or minister. My involvement with our students at H.U.C. who are studying for the Master's degree in Jewish Education indicates the social "gap" between them and their peers who study for the rabbinate. Even though they attend the same year of study in Jerusalem, and they study in the same "text" courses at the Los Angeles school, there is a perceived hierarchy of relationships from the rabbinate "downward."

During the past several years, I have taught in the Advanced Catechetical Ministries Course for the Archdiocese of Los Angeles. This program gathers Catholic laity (and some religious) who engage in family ministry, youth ministry, and Master Catechists for training in theology before they branch off into their areas of specialization. These lay-people come from their parishes in order to study theology and Scripture once a month during the first year of a two year course. In my session with them, we work together for eight hours, and they write an assignment which I grade. I discovered great enthusiasm for learning among these people. Some of them lacked extensive higher education. They were deeply interested in what a rabbi had to teach them about "Images of God in Hebrew Scripture." To my delight, their questions were well-focused and lacked traces of anti-Jewish distortions. Yet in their written work, old habits emerged. Hebrew Scripture often lapsed into New Testament quotation. The critical sharpness of their classroom questions slid off into shadow/reality distinctions between the two parts of their Scripture. Am

I disappointed? Not really. I am the only rabbi who participates in the program. Scripture represents only a small part of their studies. Other instructors in the program inform me that similar slips into old habits occur in the written assignments that they read. The participants in the program complain that the ideas they receive in their courses are not reinforced in their parishes. Their pastores do not participate in their educational concerns. The school or C.C.D. program is only one of the many claims on the pastor's time, and Jewish-Christian understanding is not central to their concerns.

Despite the hierarchies we have described, there seems to be general agreement that religious communities have a desire to perpetuate themselves. If, as we have seen, there are structural gaps in the transmission of even central, identity-affirming ideas of religious practice, how much the more so with a less central idea such as a constructive approach to Jewish-Christian relations? For to share a positive approach about either Judaism or Christianity within the church or synagogue may threaten a consensus of religious identity which proclaims *Sola Fide* (by faith alone), when it really means *Sola Fide Mea* (by my faith exclusively).[13]

Religious education, the process of becoming an integrated and mature participant in the religious community is often rooted less in history or theology than it is in ideology. In this case, ideology means a central emblem or concept which organizes whatever data enter the horizon of the participant or believer. In the domain of religion, this ideology is formed by describing what the individual is *not,* rather than by describing what the individual might *positively be.* In this sense, it is easier for a Conservative Jew to say, "I am not Reform," or for a Reform Jew to claim, "I am not Orthodox," than for either of them to articulate a positive statement of their religious identity. This same negative formulation exists among Christians. A Protestant woman in a church Sunday School class I taught on Matthew once explained Jesus' statement, "Call no man 'Father' " as meaning that Catholics were in error when they called their pastor, "Father."[14]

This need for a self-affirming/other negating ideology is most prevalent within the laity. This is comprehensible in light of the many conflicting claims upon Jewish and Christian laity. Their lives are filled with domestic conflict, struggle in the market place, and striving after their own internalized goals. Activity within the religious community provides a source of solace and enrichment. It provides structures which will ensure the survival of their religious community. While theologians speak of religious life as an opportunity for self-transformation, many lay-people look to their religious bodies to provide them with self-replication.

In the Jewish community the need for self-replication has become an obsession. The common question among Jews is no longer, "Will your children be Jewish?" but "Will your grandchildren be Jewish?" In light of demographic studies, there appears to be a basis for these concerns. However, this obsession with survival creates an outlook which is focused on the challenges of keeping people within the Jewish community, and precludes serious attention to educating them about other faiths.[15]

Let me illustrate this internal focus by describing a recent event in Los Angeles. I received a telephone call inviting me to a meeting of Jewish laity who wanted to develop an action strategy to combat the "Religious Right." My first question was, "What is our organization doing with respect to positive contacts with Christians? Do we have contact with other Christian groups who might share our concerns?" My colleague agreed that this would be an interesting approach to the problem. At the meeting, it became clear that neither the laity nor my rabbinical colleagues had any notion of the complex denominational structure of American Christianity; nor did they begin to understand the fragmentation among those groups about political views. They were, however, interested in learning. As the complexity of the issue emerged, the group reconsidered taking action. The group agreed that, at this time in history, dialogue between Jews of Orthodox and Liberal persuasion was of much greater concern than dialogue with the Christian community about the Religious Right.

The conclusion of this group did not bother me. What I found disturbing was their enthusiasm at the outset to engage themselves in a defense strategy which they perceived as exclusively Jewish. When they learned how complex the issue was—even from a Christian perspective—they found no further will to engage in the project.

In order for Judaeo-Christian studies, as they were defined in the first Bronstein Colloquium, to have an impact on the laity of either faith community, we must be able to make statements of affirmation about our own identity *and* the identity of the other. Yet, to make a statement of affirmation about Christians or Christianity is a very difficult thing for most Jews.

Many Jews claim that an affirmation of Christianity is very difficult because of the long negative history of the relationship between our two communities. However, I would claim that those who proclaim this opinion base themselves far more on ideology than upon history. Indeed, historical studies can be a good corrective for theology. From the Christian perspective we can observe how helpful Yves Congar, Avery Dulles and Edward Schillebeeckx have been in clarifying theological concepts through historical investigation. However, Salo Baron's call for an end to the "lachrymose view" of Jewish history, and Ellis Rivkin's generations of lectures about Jewish history have not moved the Jewish community beyond Heinrich Graetz's historiography of *Leidensgeschichte* (History of Tragedy) and *Gelehrtengeschichte* (History of Scholars). Tragedy and scholars resonate deeply in our Jewish sense of self. I believe that Judaeo-Christian studies can operate as an arena for this self-transformation. It can bring Jews as well as Christians to a new reading of their own traditions.[16]

B. God Requires the Heart: Self-Transformation in Theory and Practice

In this section of the paper I would like to address an area which often blocks the dialectical nature of theory and practice in the area of Jewish-Christian relations. My intention is to speak from within a Jewish context. From the perspective of most Jews, Jewish-Christian relations represent a peripheral area of concern. This is because, at its best, Judaeo-Christian studies affirm the identity of one community by affirming the identity of the other community. History, language, and experience have militated against that type of affirmation. It is important to recall, however, that some Christians and some Jews have been able to make such an affirmation about the religion of the "other."

It may be salutary at this point to define what I mean by "affirmation of the other." In some discussion between Christians and Jews there was an opinion held that each community could make concessions about their views of one another. Christians might affirm the validity of the Jewish covenant. Jews might reclaim Jesus. This "negotiation" is not what I mean by affirmation.[17] Rather, I envision affirmation as the positive assent to the consistency of a religious tradition to bring about self-transformation and self-transcendence of those who are its adherents. It is, in a sense, an aesthetic judgment which allows for a response of affirmation to an entire system. I think that affirmation of this nature is necessary for a healthy relationship between theory and practice in Jewish-Christian relations. It would ensure the integrity of each tradition, and would demand understanding, empathy and appreciation, rather than adoption or assimilation of the other tradition.[18]

A number of Christians have been able to make an affirmation of this type about Jews and Judaism. In many cases history has served as the purgation of ideology. The road to respecting Judaism as a living tradition which is rich throughout the ages, and continues to grow, began with an examination of this historical situation.[19]

Few Jews have been able to make an affirmation of Christianity. Samuel Sandmel was among those who appreciated Christianity. Much can still be gained from his frank and honest comments in *We Jews and You Christians.* However, most Jews simply cannot find examples in history which might change their point of view. To demonstrate that Frederick II held a synod in the thirteenth century which condemned the blood libel, and that Pope Innocent IV did the same, would have little impact on most Jews because the blood libel charge continued into the twentieth century. Kenneth Stow's revelation that Jews during the medieval period had a profound understanding of papal power, and utilized it to their advantage, becomes lost in light of later exercises of temporal power against the Jews in the papal states.[20]

If we as Jews could understand that Christians have conceived of their role as both criticizing the society in which they lived as well as identifying with its excesses and repressions, we might move toward affirmation. If we could comprehend the nature of Christian social criticism and it subtlety, we might find ourselves moved toward affirmation. These concepts, however, would call upon us to move beyond our knowledge of Christianity from the outside and move toward discussion with Christians who are learned in their traditions.

What type of affirmations could Jews make? An experiment would be to challenge ourselves with affirmations made about Judaism by a Christian who has learned our tradition. Could we make the same affirmations about Christianity that she has made about Judaism? In her article, "Questions Which Touch Upon the Heart of Our Faith," Mary C. Boys claims,

> The essence of good teaching lies in the ability to pose questions. In this sense Judaism has become one of Christianity's most significant

> teachers because its continued existence and vitality poses questions which touch on the heart of our faith. Simply by virtue of the fact that Israel lives, Christians must take a long hard look at our familiar formulations.[21]

Twenty years do not make up for nineteen hundred. However, we have seen more and more clearly that many Christians are attempting to pose radical questions about the society in which all of us live. They are willing, more and more, to take daring action. In the light of this public and visible change, what reformulations might we Jews make?

Could we say with Mary Boys that, "The relationship between Judaism and Christianity is a relationship between two living traditions?"[22] We Jews, of course, never claimed to have superseded Christianity, to blot it from the record of our memory, or to appropriate its traditions as our own without giving proper credit. But, in another sense, are we prepared to acknowledge that Christianity has constantly evolved; that is has a rich intellectual tradition; that it involves faith, commitment, and ethical demands upon its adherents?

Can we affirm with Mary Boys that, "Judaism and Christianity are ways of life of two peoples whose desire to be faithful to the covenant has led them down different paths to the same God."[23] For Jews as well as Christians, this is a radical reformulation. Are we modern Jews prepared to affirm Christians as a covenant people? This is a vital step in developing a praxis of Jewish-Christian relations. It is an irony that many Jews have utilized the "success" of Jewish-Christian dialogue as a paradigm for intra-Jewish dialogue. My response to them is to assert that until Christians were prepared to grant "completeness" to Judaism, no truly meaningful dialogue could occur. The reason it does not occur more often may well have to do with Jewish inability to affirm Christianity as a covenant open to God.

"To reject, however, this reductionist portrayal of Judaism necessarily entails a different, constructive task: expressing a covenant theology which honors the uniqueness and values of both ways of life."[24] Mary Boys' polemic against reductionist portrayals should strike deeply at those of us who hear or read simplistic descriptions of Christianity. We are challenged to build a constructive theology which expresses the uniqueness of Christianity. Such a work would balance some of the heavy emphasis on the negative polarity of Jewish-Christian relations.[25] It would explain in terms that Jews could understand how Christians view their religion as a force for self-transcendence.[26]

Jewish affirmations of Christianity in the sense that I have explained it may prepare us for the need to part with some of our current images of dialogue. One of the images which Jews have held is that of asymmetry. They emphasize that Christians are impelled to dialogue from theology; Jews come to dialogue because of history.[27] To a certain extent, I think, that may have been true. It accounts for the lack of communication between Jews and Christians in the initial stages of their dialogues. However, it would appear that Christians have recently come to dialogue with a sophisticated political and historical agenda. In the case of the National Conference of Catholic Bishops, their historical/political agenda is often grounded in theology and traditional sources. The Jewish community may pay a price for continuing to hold fast to its previous images of Christians who come to dialogue.

Archbishop Roger Mahony of Los Angeles recently addressed the leadership of the American Jewish Committee and the Jewish Federation-Council. He stated:

> The questions of the State of Israel, the Holocaust and Anti-Semitism would certainly rank high on the Jewish agenda. Dialogue has brought the Roman Catholic community to know and respect that. Abortion, Church-State issues and immigrant issues would rank high on the Roman Catholic agenda. I believe that this is known in the Jewish community.
>
> What can we do about these differing agenda items? We can surely attempt to become more informed about and sensitive to the concerns of the other. We can move when movement is possible. We can discard old objections when they no longer apply.
>
> What should we not do about differing agenda items? We should not see them as obstructionist ploys. We should not make the compliance of the other a litmus test for dialogue. We should not refuse the right and legitimacy of the other to raise these concerns again and again in dialogue.[28]

I have quoted the Archbishop's speech at length because I believe it represents the next stage in the dialogue. It will be exciting and challenging. Without a more profound understanding of Christianity—its history, traditions, and its capacity for dynamic growth—we may become mired in the old agenda.

There is another area for growth in theory and practice of Judaeo-Christian studies. This area is Religious Education. Much constructive work has occurred during the last thirty years with respect to religious school textbooks. The American Jewish Committee can take pride in its sponsorship of textbook surveys of Christian religious education.[29] What about Jewish textbooks? The one study of Jewish textbooks which was done reports that there was relatively little prejudicial portrayal of the outgroup. However, the study found less attention to the out-group.[30] We might conclude that Christians and Moslems are generally absent from Jewish textbooks, and, when they are presented, there is some prejudicial stereotyping. A study by one of our graduate students on a recently published textbook of Jewish history indicated serious distortions of Christians and Christianity both in the period of Late Antiquity and the Middle Ages. Professor Gavin Langmuir of Stanford University published a study of the image of Judaism in college level textbooks on the medieval period. Not surprisingly, he discovered that Jews were generally characterized as usurers, and very much underrepresented. Langmuir also studied the images of Christians and Christianity in Jewish history books. His work revealed that Christians and other "out-groups" are presented as illiterates who did little else than persecute Jews. Jewish authors frequently cite Langmuir's work on Jews in Christian textbooks; they rarely cite his article on the presentation of Christians in Jewish books.[31]

Two years ago, John Carmody wrote about "Judaism vis à vis Christianity: How to Make Changes." This study indicated that many Christian educators expressed dissatisfaction with the treatment of Judaism in the religious education material available to them. Carmody indicated that the place to attack the problem was at the level of the publisher and the author. He suggested that guidelines be set by each publisher for how Jews ought to be portrayed. It was also recommended that Christian publishers attempt to hire Jewish readers for their textbooks. This is already the case with some Christian publishers. Carmody also suggested, "This might also be the point at which reciprocity—Christian readers for Jewish materials might be a matter to investigate."[32] An informal survey of publishers of Jewish textbooks indicated that none of them had Christian readers or advisors.

But textbooks are not the only problem in moving toward new images of one another. Mary Boys has suggested, "Production of materials alone will not lead to changes. No material is teacher-proof. Because teachers are mediators of knowledge and not mere automatons, they need to be given time to rework their own understanding. One wonders how much effort has been expended in remediating an adequate theology of Judaism for Christian educators."[33] John Carmody proposes that publishers provide for teams of Jewish and Christian scholars to do in-service training for religious educators.[34] My colleagues on the faculty of the Rhea Hirsch School of Education at the Los Angeles campus of Hebrew Union College indicate that far more time is spent within Jewish religious schools on textbooks than on teacher training. When training does occur, it customarily focuses on *techniques* rather than on the *Weltanschauung* of the individual teacher.[35]

The changes which we seek in Jewish-Christian relations will not occur through changing educational materials. These changes are occurring and they are significant. However, we must not forget that the change must also occur within the individual. The Talmud reminds us, *Rachmana Liba Ba'ey*—God requires the heart (*Sanhedrin* 106b). We must never confuse *praxis* with *techne*; and we must never separate *theoria* from *praxis.* They exist in a dialectical relationship to one another. A Christian who does not believe that Judaism is a covenant on-going with God cannot transmit a positive image of Judaism to students, parishioners, or anyone else. A Jew who identifies the Christian religion exclusively with perpetrators of violence against Jews and Judaism can never effectively teach much more than civil conduct toward Christians—and the only motivation for that conduct will be to prevent harm to themselves, not because they view in the other human being an *imago dei.* Separation of theory and practice at the deep structure level can account for the dissonance between authoritative teaching and religious education or pulpit preaching.

C. *Darkhe Shalom*: Pathways to the Future

We have described three publics for the transmission of a religious tradition: the clergy who are trained in the seminary; the teachers in the church or synagogue who come from the laity; and the laity itself. We have argued that a change can occur within these groups when there is a mutual affirmation of one another toward a common end. In this third section of the paper we will describe some examples of projects which embody parts of this change. In each example we will discern the opportunity for individuals to present themselves and their tradition within the context of the other tradition. Sensitivity and communication grow out of a mutual need to understand and to be understood.

The intense parochialism of seminary training poses a problem for many students. They come from a world where specificity is diffused through many activities and relationships. In their seminary, they live in close quarters with the texts of their religious tradition. The frenetic pace of training forces them to spend most of their time in course work or in field placement. Intrusions into the few moments of leisure time are measured against a very strict scale of justice.

It was this reality that brought about the St. John's Seminary-Hebrew Union College exchange. We knew that a speaker during lunch or after dinner would have little impact at St. John's or Hebrew Union College. Therefore, professors visit classes within the other institution. We also live the life of each place. Rabbis attend the Liturgy of the Hours, the Eucharistic celebration, and even moments of devotion. I am probably one of the few non-Catholics who have witnessed the Benediction of the Real Presence during the Lenten season. Priests attend the synagogue service at Hebrew Union College; sit in the lounge during coffee breaks; and make themselves available for private meetings. We have taught Liturgy at each other's school, Homiletics, New Testament, Sacramental Theology, Medieval Bible Commentaries, and History. The professor of Scripture from St. John's has taught the development of the exegetical tradition on the second Psalm from its ancient Near Eastern origins through the Middle Ages. The professor of Jewish History has spoken about the utilization of prophetic texts within Jewish homilies. Questions from both student bodies are intensely personal. Most important is that rabbis and priests come to view education from the other tradition as a natural part of their seminary training.

I believe that the Interseminary Retreat sponsored by the National Conference of Christians and Jews in Los Angeles has been very successful in helping future Jewish and Christian clergy to integrate interreligious ideas into their reality. "Intersem," as it has come to be known, includes students from a variety of Jewish and Christian seminaries: Hebrew Union College (Reform Jewish), University of Judaism (Conservative Jewish), Fuller Theological Seminary, School of Theology at Claremont, and St.

John's. The retreat is planned entirely by students under the direction of Rev. Glen Polling, an Episcopalian priest, who protects the students from all institutional and faculty pressure.

During the retreat, each religious tradition presents a worship service with commentary. The remaining time is spent in small groups discussing themes chosen by the students. Here the seminarians reveal their prejudices and take their hurts to be healed. Catholics can explain that their church no longer sells indulgences. Protestant students become more sensitive about the species of the Eucharist. Bread and wine left on the table or brought into the dining room after the Protestant worship had the same impact on the Catholics that a Jew who observes the dietary laws would have upon being told that his "veal" was pork. Jewish seminarians often observe Christian worship for the first time in their lives. They come to learn that there is more to being a Christian than coming down the aisle. They learn that they share similar aspirations for redemption of the world and themselves. It is significant that they become acquainted with each other's language of religious expression.

Students at Hebrew Union College become quite bonded to their Catholic colleagues. In one case, a student's bi-weekly pulpit and a young deacon's assignment were in the same city. The deacon showed up every Friday night for worship bringing some of his flock along. Eventually, the Jews in the community gathered in the church, where Catholic worship was explained to them. It was the first time that many Jews and Catholics had experienced each other's worship.

Students are not alone in their need for interfaith understanding. Faculty require it as well. When I returned to Los Angeles after the first Bronstein Colloquium, I called upon the support of another participant, James A. Sanders. Together with a group of other professors we organized a retreat under the sponsorship of the American Jewish Committee. We wanted to avoid the atmosphere of a scholarly colloquium. Therefore, we had small groups where we spoke out of our own experience. The attendance came from Catholic, Protestant and Jewish seminaries. Our focus was on two questions: 1) What do we teach about the other's tradition? 2) What can we learn from one another about training the religious leadership of tomorrow?

It became clear how profoundly dedicated we were as seminary faculty to our respective religious bodies. However, we did feel the deep yearning to be very much a part of the scholarly world associated with the university. No one was totally satisfied with a sense of balance. However, there was a growing restlessness with the perception of ourselves exclusively within the university tradition. All of us present resonanted to Edward Farley's idea that *theologia* as *studium* ought not to be separated from *theologia* as *habitus animae.*[36] What we were striving for was an integrity of scholarship, teaching, and living, which is best understood under the formula attributed to St. Benedict, *Laborare est orare* (to work is to pray). As we spoke from the unique vocabularies of our traditions, we became aware of the common structures of our work.

We have observed occasions where seminary students and seminary faculty have had the opportunity to engage in mutual affirmation. What about the religious educators who are not part of seminary training? What about the laity? This is our weakest, and paradoxically, our most important area for development. Let me, then, describe a new project which may tie these threads together. I believe that a description of this project reflects the move from the old agenda (dialogue as didactic or pedagogic) to the new agenda (dialogue as conversation or androgogic).

The project began in 1981, when a local rabbi and priest who had long been active in interfaith work approached the Hebrew Union College to supply speakers for courses in religion at local Catholic high schools. We then made arrangements for the students who had spoken to attend a meeting at the College together with the teachers from the high schools. At the meeting, we suggested that Jews and Judaism might well spiral through the entire curriculum of the high school in such diverse courses as literature, history, and government. Six months later, we met again, and one of the supervising teachers made a request for speakers in the diverse areas we had originally suggested. At this point we realized that we might consolidate "speakers" into a single teaching internship for a graduate student. This student would spend five hours per week under the supervision of a master teacher. Our student would attend faculty orientations, departmental meetings, and participate in the "life" of the institution. At Hebrew Union College, each student intern would meet with members of the faculty in order to reflect on his or her experiences.

Our students have given lessons in literature, history, and in such diverse courses as marriage preparation and family life. They have participated in retreats for students and faculty. Anecdotes about their experience indicate that they have reached the young people both on an intellectual and affective level. In one school an intern helped the student council develop a Holocaust commemoration week. Another intern had the opportunity to address the C.C.D. Conference of the Archdiocese of Los Angeles. The common experience of all the students has been that they went to teach, but they have been taught far more. As a result of presenting their faith within another context, they have come to examine their own tradition from new perspectives.

To enrich this internship experience, our students are joined by student interns from St. John's seminary. They are in the high schools on the same day each week. They meet together with the master teacher and plan joint activities. I am sure that much informal sharing about seminary life goes on as well. In this program, seminary, teacher, and lay community meet. We have moved from the demand for speakers and more educational material to the demands by the speakers for further education—to study in order to teach.

A memorandum from our final meeting with the students this year will chart our growth. Students have called for: 1) an orientation for all student interns with their supervising teachers and the principal of the school to take place at the Hebrew Union College; 2) a seminar on Catholic sacraments; 3) a full bibliography on Catholicism. These demands indicate that the students have grown from people who have something to teach into people who want to communicate effectively to those whom they teach. In order to accomplish this goal, they recognize that they must be able to affirm the community with whom they will share their experiences.

In each of these activities we have observed the opportunity for dialogue to create an atmosphere which is open to self-transformation and self-transcendence. Mary Boys uses the term, "passing over." She borrows this term from John Dunne's book, *The Way of All the Earth.* It describes the process of shifting one's standpoint in order to go over to another's culture, way of life, or religion. A second movement follows, "coming home," that is, returning with new insight into one's own culture, way of life or religion. Theory and practice can exist in dialectical tension only if both parties are willing to "pass over" and "come back."[37]

What language will enable us to make this passage safely? What model can we utilize so that we can maintain our tradition, affirm the other with empathy, and then return to our own? I believe that David Tracy's model of the analogical imagination can serve us well.

Analogical language, as Tracy defines it, is a language of ordered relationships articulating similaries in difference. It is in pressing toward similarities in difference that we can achieve our most productive work. If laity, teachers, and clergy can understand similarities in difference, then no one's integrity need be violated. We may speak of what is familiar to us and observe analogies in the experience of others. We shall not mistake those analogies for identities. However, we shall understand that they are inextricably and powerfully linked as one community is linked to the other.

How can we provide the bonds so that links can be forged? Tracy offers us the model of conversation. We must be speaking with one another, debating, and arguing. Closer contact is required at all levels for similarites in difference to emerge. Willingness to "pass over" must be rooted in the security that we can come back to our roots.[38]

The world grows larger around us. We recognize that the ways of the West are no longer the ways of the world. The human family reflected from our satellites is neither Jewish nor Christian. From this perspective we have more in common than we perhaps ever thought possible before. Theory and practice unite ideal and real. We can hold the image as we work to craft our world.

Notes

1. Barry Cytron, "On Not Speaking to Christians—Ever," *Sh'ma: A Journal of Jewish Responsibility* 16:302 (November, 1985), pp. 11–12

2. Samuel Sandmel, "Antiquarianism versus Contemporaneity: The Relevance of Studies in Religion," in *Two Living Traditions* (Detroit: 1972), pp. 20–27

3. Alfred Gottschalk, "*Nostra Aetate*: A Twenty Year Perspective," Address delivered 20 October 1985, in Cincinnati, Ohio.

4. See my study, "The *Speculum Ecclesiae* by Honorius Augustodensis on Jews and Judaism: Preaching at Regensburg in the Twelfth Century," in E. Du Bruck and K. H. Goller (eds.), *Crossroads of Medieval Civilization: The City of Regensburg and its Intellectual Milieu* (Michigan: 1983). An example of the possible use of medieval imagery for paradigms of contemporary Jewish-Christian relations would be my essay, "*Speculum Concilii:* Through the Mirror Brightly," in Roger Brooks, ed.: *Twenty Years After Vatican II: Unanswered Questions and Unquestioned Answers* (Notre Dame, IN: Notre Dame University Press, 1987).

5. David Tracy, *The Analogical Imagination* (New York: 1981), p. 35. I have also found an excellent formulation of the problem in Mary C. Boys, "The Role of Theology in Religious Education," *Horizons* 11:1 (1984), pp. 61–85

6. The term "public" here follows the use by David Tracy in *The Analogical Imagination,* pp. 1–46. It is helpful for a description of the nature of discourse between learners and teachers. I believe that much of the work in Jewish-Christian relations is rhetorical in the classical sense of the word. We are attempting to persuade people that their understanding of Judaism or Christianity must be changed. Before we can develop a language of dialogue, we must be sensitive to the structures of discourse which have preceded our own. We might then develop persuasive discourse for our own time. A fine example of rhetorical analysis of anti-Jewish discourse in the ancient world would be Robert L. Wilkin, *John Chrysostom and the Jews* (Berkeley: 1983). A. Lukyn Williams, *Adversus Judaeos* (Cambridge: 1935), reognized that rhetoric was crucial to changing the anti-Jewish animus among Christians. However, his own evangelical spirit obscured the clarity of his argument.

7. H. N. Bialik, *"Metei Midbar," Kol Kitbe H. N. Bialik* (Tel Aviv: 1965), pp. 92–95

8. Daniel Jeremy Silver, "The Core of Our Calling: Who is a Rabbi? What is a Rabbi? Why is a Rabbi?" *Journal of Reform Judaism* 33:1 (1986), pp. 1–14, indicates this hierarchy. Silver does not consider the pulpit rabbi a "scholar" and indicates that this title is more appropriate to Judaic Studies faculties in secular universities. Silver does not ascribe any significance to the seminary professor. He claims that "Seminary training has a reputation 'down there' with teacher training (3)." For evidence of hierarchy and tensions in Christian seminary training, one should consult Joseph C. Hough and John Cobb, *Christian Identity and Theological Education* (Chico, California: 1985) and Paul M. Van Buren, "Theological Education for the Church's Relationship to the Jewish People," *Journal of Ecumenical Studies* 21:3 (1984), pp. 489–505

9. Although I have described this ecology in hierarchical terms, I do not believe that a hierarchy provides the ideal ecological system. I do not believe that any person should be a transmitter of knowledge without the constant possibility for transformation. In an ideal setting, each group would be open to learning from another group. However, the need to claim territory or authority seems to invade most human systems. Silver's article cited in the previous note indicates that congregational rabbis have their authority "eroded" by other professionals within the Jewish community. The conflict between theology as a discipline and religious education is brilliantly outlined by Mary C. Boys, "The Role of Theology in Religious Education," (see note 5).

10. James A. Sanders, *Canon and Community* (Philadelphia: 1984). One might also consult his paper, "The Bible and the Believing Communities," prepared for the Lilly Endowment Consultation on the Seminary and the Congregation 12 March 1985.

11. Lou H. Silberman, "Listening to the Text," *Journal of Biblical Literature* 102:1 (1983), pp. 3–26

12. John Cobb frames the question in a similar way for Protestant seminaries. Cfr. his address to the Divinity School of the University of Chicago, "Claiming the Center," *Criterion* (Winter 1986), pp. 2–8, where he rails against "discipli-nolatry" within seminary faculties.

13. There are Christians who claim that the issue of Judaism is crucial for Christian theology and religious education. Cfr. Mary C. Boys, "Questions Which Touch on the Heart of Our Faith," *Religious Education* 76:6 (1981), pp. 636–656; Clemens Thoma, *A Christian Theology of Judaism* (New York: 1980); Paul van Buren, *Discerning the Way* (New York: 1980), and *A Christian Theology of the People Israel* (New York: 1983). One of the most radical statements about the centrality of Judaism for rethinking Christian theology remains Rosemary Ruether, *Faith and Fratricide* (New York: 1974). Theologians in Germany have considered this a central issue as well. Cfr. Hans Hermann Henrix, "Der Dialog mit dem Judentum als Aufgabe oekumenischer Theologie," *Una Sancta* 31 (1976), pp. 136–145; Franz Mussner, *Traktat uber die Juden* (Munich: 1979; E. T. New York: 1984); Wilfried Schweikhardt, *Zwischen Dialog und Mission* (Berlin: 1980); Peter von der Osten-Sacken, *Katechismus und Siddur* (Berlin, 1984).

14. William B. Kennedy, "Ideology and Education: A Fresh Approach for Religious Education," *Religious Education* 80:3 (1985), pp. 331–334, provides a succinct account of the role ideology plays in religious education. The concept of "maturity" in a religious context may be somewhat alien to Jews who customarily refer to religious "maturity" as the responsibility for performing the divine commandments. My use of the term here derives from the work of Christian scholars. Cfr. Craig Dykstra, *Vision and Character* (New York: 1981); Thomas H. Groome, *Christian Religious Education* (San Francisco: 1980); James Fowler, *Stages of Faith* (New York: 1981); Kenneth Stokes (ed.), *Faith Development in the Adult Life Cycle* (New York: 1982). My colleague, Dr. Isa Aron, demonstrates why philosophers of liberal Jewish education have failed to develop a coherent philosophical structure of religious education in her article, "Is It Possible to Create a Liberal Philosophy of Religious Education?" which will be published in *Religious Education.*

15. For an account of "other-negation" Jewish identity, one should consult Harold M. Schulweis, "Antisemitism: Malignant Obsession, '*Moment* 10:6 (1985), pp. 60–62. The most widely quoted statement of the dangers of demographic demise for the Jewish people is E. Bergman, "The American Jewish Population Erosion," *Midstream* 23:8 (1977), pp. 9–19. Challenges have recently come from scholars trained in demography. Cfr. "Jews More or Less: An Interview with Steven M. Cohen," *Moment* 4:6 (1979), pp. 11–14; and Bruce M. Phillips, "Intermarriage, Fertility, and Jewish Survival: New Evidence from the 80's," *Contemporary Jewry Annual* 8 (1986), forthcoming. The most negative formulation of Jewish identity *vis à vis* Christianity was made by Joseph Soloveitchik, "Confrontation," *Tradition*

6 (1964), pp. 5–29, who believes that issues of theology can be discussed only by members of the same covenantal bond. Their religious language is so private that it is unintelligible to anyone outside their own religious experience. This position was restated by David Berger, "Jewish-Christian Relations: A Jewish Perspective," *Journal of Ecumenical Studies* 20:1 (1983), pp. 5–32, in the broader context of positive developments in non-theological areas. Berger stressed the importance of the Orthodox Jewish perspective on matters of social concern for Jewish Christian relations.

16. Henry Siegman, "Dialogue with Christians: A Jewish Dilemma," *Judaism* 20:1 (1971), pp. 93–102, articulates the notion of asymmetry in Jewish-Christian dialogue. For the use of tradition as a corrective in theological studies, one should consult Yves Congar, *Tradition and Traditions* (New York: 1967); Avery Dulles, *Models of the Church* (New York: 1978) and *Models of Revelation* (New York: 1985); Edward Schillebeeckx, *Jesus: An Experiment in Christology* (New York: 1981), and *Christ: The Experience of Jesus as Lord* (New York: 1981). In biblical theology, one should read the works of Raymond Brown who demonstrates the compatibility of contemporary biblical-critical scholarship with the *Magisterium* of the Catholic Church. Cfr. *Biblical Exegesis and Church Doctrine* (New York: 1985). For Jewish perspectives on history and ideology, see H. Graetz, *The Structures of Jewish History* (New York: 1975); S. Baron, *History and Jewish Historians* (New York: 1964); E. Rivkin, *The Shaping of Jewish History* (New York: 1971). A searching approach to the dimensions of Jewish historical writing and its impact on Jewish identity is to be found in Josef Yerushalmi, *Zakhor: Jewish History and Jewish Memory* (Seattle: 1982).

17. For Jewish views of Christianity which represent attempts to reclaim Jesus, see Donald Hagner, *The Jewish Reclamation of Jesus: An Analysis and Critique of the Modern Study of Jesus* (Grand Rapids, Michigan: 1983). A more general presentation of Jewish views on Christianity is to be found in Walter Jacob, *Christianity Through Jewish Eyes* (Cincinnati: 1974). Jacob correctly emphasizes that Jews have tended to understand Christianity through the lens of scholarly disciplines rather than through theological reflection.

18. I acknowledge that the term "affirmation" in the context of this paper needs further development. I do believe that my use of affirmation as an aesthetic judgment comports with David Tracy's analogical imagination which is the model for Part Three of this paper. Two essays in the volume *Learning and Teaching: The Ways of Knowing,* Yearbook of the National Society for the Study of Education 84 (Chicago: 1985) have been most helpful: Elliot Eisner, "Aesthetic Modes of Knowing," pp. 23–56; and Dwayne Hubner, "Spirituality and Knowing," pp. 159–173.

19. Franklin Littell, *The Crucifixion of the Jews* (New York: 1975); A. Roy and Alice Eckhart, *Elder and Younger Brothers* (New York: 1967). These scholars utilize the Holocaust as a purgation of previous ideas about Judaism. See note 13 above for other scholars who utilize other historical events in the history of

Jewish-Christian relations as the basis for their revised Christian theologies of Judaism.

20. Samuel Sandmel, *We Jews and You Christians* (Philadelphia: 1967). Salo Baron, "Plenitude of Apostolic Powers and Medieval Jewish Serfdom," in L. Feldman (ed.), *Ancient and Medieval Jewish History: Essays by Salo Wittmayer Baron* (New Brunswick, New Jersey: 1972) pp. 284–307. Kenneth Stow, *The '1007 Anonymous' and Papal Sovereignty: Jewish Perceptions of the Papacy and Papal Power in the High Middle Ages* (Cincinnati: 1984).

21. Mary C. Boys, *"Questions,"* (see note 13), p. 626.

22. *Ibid.*, p. 645.

23. *Ibid.*, p. 646.

24. *Ibid.*, p. 647.

25. An excellent and constructive model for developing appropriate Jewish responses to Christians and Christianity may be found in J. Sternfield (ed.), *Homework for Jews: Preparing for Jewish-Christian Dialogue* (National Conference of Christians and Jews: 1985).

26. I am aware that many scholars claim that systematic theology is "alien" to Judaism as a mode of discourse for explanation. I am unwilling to eliminate such thinkers as Hermann Cohen or Kaufmann Kohler from the ranks of those who developed a mode of discourse appropriate to the explanation of Judaism. It is clear that a new hermeneutical movement is developing with respect to classical Jewish sources and their presentation to a Western-educated Jewish lay audience. Cfr. Barry Holtz (ed.), *Back to the Sources* (New York: 1984). See also the important review by William Cutter in *Modern Judaism* 5:3 (1985), pp. 301–311. The literary efforts of Jakob Petuchowski and Eugene Borowitz may continue to lead us to a more fully developed Jewish theological exposition of Christianity. Borowitz's *Contemporary Christologies: A Jewish Response* (New York: 1980) offers a sympathetic and affirmative treatment of Christian thought.

27. Michael J. Cook, "Envisioning a New Symmetry in Jewish-Christian Dialogue," in J. Petuchowski (ed.), *Defining a Discipline: The Aims and Objectives of Judaeo-Christian Studies,* Proceedings of the first Sol and Arlene Bronstein Colloquium in Judaeo-Christian Studies (Cincinnati: 1984), pp. 88–101.

28. Archibishop Roger Mahony, "Jewish-Catholic Dialogue in Los Angeles," *Origins* 15:30 (9 January 1986) pp. 500–502

29. For bibliographical information on the various textbooks' studies, see Mary C. Boys, "Questions," pp. 639–640, notes 9–15. A full-length study of the problem is provided in Eugene Fisher, *Faith and Prejudice* (New York: 1977).

30. Bernard D. Weinryb and Daniel Garnick, *Jewish School Textbooks and Intergroup Relations* (American Jewish Committee: 1972).

31. Gavin Langmuir, "Majority History and Post-Biblical Jews," *Journal of the History of Ideas* 27:3 (1966), pp. 343–364; "Tradition, History and Prejudice," *Jewish Social Studies* 30:3 (1980), pp. 157–168. Langmuir's writings on medieval anti-Semitism are the most cogent, clear and free of apologetics that exist. It is a pity that he is not more widely read by "experts" in anti-Semitism.

32. John Carmody, "Judaism vis à vis Christianity: How to Make Changes," *Journal of Ecumenical Studies* 21:3 (1984), pp. 507–522.

33. Mary C. Boys, "Questions," p. 645

34. John Carmody, "Judaism," pp. 520–521

35. Sara S. Lee, "In-Service Education: A Priority for All Seasons," *The Pedagogic Reporter* 35:2 (1984), pp. 22–23

36. Edward Farley, *Theologia: The Fragmentation and Unity of Theological Education* (Philadelphia: 1983)

37. Mary C. Boys, "Questions," p. 637, quoting John Dunne, *The Way of All the Earth* (New York: 1972), p. ix

38. David Tracy, *The Analogical Imagination* (see note 5), pp. 405–456, offers the most challenging model for dialogue. It is pluralistic in both its assumptions and actions, because it relates to the concept of creative reinterpretation of religious classics. My experience in dialogue indicates that study of the sacred texts of our traditions in each other's presence elicits very positive and fruitful responses.

Part III

The Joint Study of Scripture

RONALD M. HALS

6. *Some Aspects of the Exegesis of Jeremiah 31:31–34*

Preface

The new covenant text is a much treated one. Whole books are devoted to it regularly. Christoph Levin recently spent 279 pages in *Die Verheissung des neuen Bundes* (FRLANT 137; Goettingen: Vandenhoeck & Ruprecht, 1985). I have chosen to deal yet one more time with such previously worked over material, not because I have something original to say, but because I feel that the differences between the exegesis done by Jews and Christians are likely to become visible here, and in point of fact have often done so. (I shall use the grossly over-simplified terminology "Jews and Christians" solely as a convenient abbreviation, being nonetheless aware that such generalizations could be misunderstood as demeaning stereotypes.) As a Christian presenter, my focus will be on where and why efforts by Christians to expound this passage are likely to take on a distinctively Christian character. This concentration will result in a deliberate distortion of the balance of a normal exegetical study. I believe such a distortion is appropriate and even necessary for the purposes of this Colloquium. If a more standard, undistorted pattern were followed, I would be imposing on you the task of ferreting out in the discussion what the differences were, and thereby making the actual analysis of those differences delayed and complicated. Because I believe the analysis of the differences to be the most significant part of our joint task, I shall present only enough of the exegetical "common ground" to make the treatment of the differences understandable. In this I shall attempt to be as frank and honest as possible, but my listeners will need to be alert for those places where my own ignorance and unconscious prejudices lead me to inaccuracies of fact and/or misjudgments in analyzing causes.

It is important to make one final preliminary observation about the underlying context within which biblical study takes place. In the Kaiser-Kuemmel *Exegetical Method,* this statement appears on the very first page: "In the final analysis all theological endeavor serves as a preparation for the proclamation of the gospel" (New York: Seabury, 1967). This is a sort of shorthand way of saying that within a certain tradition (roughly German Protestantism) the Bible is subjected to intense and disciplined study because of the conviction that, when dealing with this body of literature, one experiences the phenomena of finding oneself addressed and being a part of a community that shares that experience. This is not some sort of special mysticism nor some kind of litmus test able or needing to be reaffirmed regularly, but rather an affirmation by a conscious insider within a particular tradition. It is what underlies the custom of preaching and preparation for preaching within that tradition, and it is obviously a generalization of only limited value and relevance. Still, it is the reason why in most of Protestantism the exegesis of a biblical text is usually done within a framework which is rooted in a tradition of sermon preparation. This is still—at least in a theoretical way—characteristic of the practice in German universities. While one may excerpt certain parts of the process of exegesis, and find them to be purely objective and scientific, that should in no way obscure the fact that exegesis as a whole exists within a larger framework. Emil Fackenheim, in "New Hearts and the Old Covenant" (*The Divine Helmsman,* ed. by James L. Crenshaw and Samuel Sandmel; New York: Ktav, 1980, pp. 195–196), writes of the need for all such pre-reflective understandings to become as fully self-conscious as possible. He compares the comments of Artur Weiser and Yehezqel Kaufmann on Jer. 31:31–34 and finds them both lacking in this regard.

Exegesis of the Text Proper

Where does one begin an exegesis? Theoretically one insists on the hermeneutical circle, and claims that every part of an exegesis must continually be revised in the light of every other part. Practically one chooses to begin somewhere, and thereby reveals about oneself what one finds to be basic. I begin with form, because I am a form critic, that is, one who finds an analysis of form to be of fundamental importance. Jews do not frequently follow this path, but this is essentially just a matter of the extent of a recent German heritage in one's training.

Jer. 31:31–34 in response to the question "What is it?" reveals itself to belong to the broad category "prophecy of salvation (Heil)," and to the subcategory "portrayal of salvation," and to the narrower subcategory "portrayal by means of contrast to a former order." The formula *hinneh yamim ba-im* ("behold, days are coming") introduces in several places a contrast in "times" (Levin, p. 24). In Jer. 16:14–15 and its parallel 23:7–8, there is presented a contrast in the way oaths will be taken. In Jer. 31:38–40, there appears a contrast in regard to the future, rebuilt Jerusalem. Even in doom-oriented passages, like 31:27 about sour grapes, and 7:32 with its parallel 19:6 about Topheth, this contrast of times is affirmed. An examination of the contrast motif in prophecies of salvation (consolation or *tanchumim* would be a more traditional Jewish term) reveals the key significance of the word "new" for such structural analogies with the past. Rohland, (*Die Bedeutung der Erwaehlungstraditionen fuer die Eschatologie der Alttestamentlichen Propheten;* Dissertation: Heidelberg, 1956), has shown that it is primarily election traditions that are employed in this prophetic eschatology. (Note here the heavy use of words taken from Christian dogmatic tradition.) A preliminary conclusion from an examination of form points to a difference in terminology between Jews and Christians. This is only a surface matter, and is shown to be so by the way M. Weinfeld, ("Jeremiah and the Spiritual Metamorphosis of Israel," ZAW 88, 1976, pp. 17–56), moves to use the same passages, albeit with a different terminology and the inclusion of Jer. 3:16–18 (contrast about the ark), which Levin omits as later on literary-critical grounds. With the introduction of this factor, a new difference appears. Although no longer of the view "Higher criticism, higher anti-Semitism," most Jewish scholars tend not to assign such a fundamental role to literary criticism, tending to take material within a given book much more at face value, sometimes giving the impression of being non-critical. However, in the hey-day of Christian biblical studies in the 1930s to 1960s, what I consider a healthy development took place, by which the final form of the text was assigned preeminence. No longer was it acceptable to dismiss something as secondary and thereby to be discarded as inferior. Now all of a text lays equal claim on an expositor to be explained. (e.g., Zimmerli's

Ezekiel spends more time in some places on secondary parts.) Thus this difference between Jews and Christians becomes somewhat less prominent.

For convenience, here is what a form-critic's structural analysis of Jer. 31:31–34 might look like:

I. Preliminaries	31:31a
A. "Coming days" formula	31aα
B. Prophetic utterance formula	31aβ
II. Announcement as portrayal	31b–34
A. Intervention	31b
1. Affirmation of divine initiative	31bα . . .δ
2. Specification of partners, Israel and Judah	31bβγ
B. Description	32–34
1. Negatively	32
a. In general—not like the covenant with fathers at the time of Exodus	32a
b. In particular	32bαβ
1) Which they broke	32bα
2) Although I was faithful (or "And I destroyed them")	32bβ
c. Prophetic utterance formula	32bγ
2. Positively	33
a. Contrasting resumptive repetition of intervention	33aαβγδ
1) Affirmation of divine initiative	33aα
2) Specification of partner, Israel	33aβ
3) Specification of time: after those days	33aγ
4) Prophetic utterance formula	33aδ
b. Specification of contrast as continued intervention	33aεζ
1) My Torah put in their midst	33aε
2) Written on their hearts	33aζ
c. Further specification as results	33b–34abαβγ
1) Covenant formula in future tense	33b
2) Internal transformation	34abαβγ
a) Contrasting former order: no more teaching to know Yahweh	34a
b) Reason making new order different: all shall know me	34bαβ
3) Prophetic utterance formula	34bγ
d. Concluding explanatory intervention	34bδε
1) Positively: forgive iniquity	34bδ
2) Negatively: not remember sin	34bε

This structural analysis bears out the claim that the text's central focus is on the contrast between the new covenant with the old. Thus the key question becomes: What's new about the new covenant? The text deals repeatedly with that question. (1) In v. 31 an initial element of newness is mentioned in passing, when both Israel and Judah are specified, but the mention in v. 32 of Exodus and the reference in v. 33 to Israel as the designation of the covenant partner make it plain that what is in mind here is a return to the situation of one Israel in the time before Jeroboam I. (2) In v. 32 the newness is approached negatively, when it is pointed out that what was wrong with the first covenant was the people's disobedience. At this point we begin to notice a developing problem: If the previous flaw was only in the people's disobedience, that is not really a part of the covenant itself, and so how could a new covenant cure that flaw? (3) In v. 33 precisely the question of what is new is dealt with, as a description of newness is given which does not hint at any sort of change in the Torah as the expression of the covenant, but promises solely a change in the means by which the divine will reaches the human partners. In a passing contrast, which is not further developed, there is promised a writing of the Torah upon the hearts of the people—presumably, although not said, in contrast to something written upon stone tablets. This results in a covenant relationship of peoplehood expressed in the future tense. (4) In v. 34 the dramatic results of newness are portrayed as the lack of any further need for teaching the knowledge of God, for the entire people will be characterized by this newness, as a result of the action of divine forgiveness.

Obviously it is in vv. 33–34 that the newness is specified, and the history of exegetical efforts reveals a host of attempts to understand just wherein the newness consists. Recent study of the passage has tended to be guided by the light shed on these verses by two things: (1) the context of other messages of hope within Jeremiah, and (2) the context of the entire prophetic proclamation. Within the Book of Jeremiah, the key passages are 24:7 and 32:38–41. What those passages have in common with 31:31–34 is the affirmation that the Lord will transform the will (heart) of His people, so that as a result of the transformation, obedience will be automatic, i.e., built in. Helga Weippert prefers to say "instinctive" ('Das Wort vom Neuen Bund in Jeremia xxi 31–34," VT 29, 1979, pp. 336–351). This is for many a most unwelcome idea, raising the specter of robot-like, captive wills (which automatically implies automata!) of the type that can only bring to mind those repulsive dolls with internal recordings operated by pulling a string, so that one is subjected to a nauseatingly unending repetition of a phrase such as "I love you." In a Dropsie College dissertation on Jer. 31:31–34, Frank Seilhamer came indeed to the conclusion that this passage, properly understood, is truly a dismal one, one which abandons hope in the possibility of human repentance (New World Press, 1976). In any case, the thought of programmed obedience is certainly a cold contrast to the warmth suggested by more romantic notions about the passage, which confine the newness to the contrast between inwardness and externality.

Unfortunately, the examination of other prophetic literature seems convincingly to bear out this understanding of the newness as consisting in the transformation of the wills of God's people. Ezek. 36:26–27 says nearly the exact same thing in only a slightly different formulation, when it speaks of a new heart and a new spirit which will "cause you to walk in my statutes." But the whole worry about a loss of human freedom is actually a misplaced one. I think my good friend Frank Seilhamer has as little need to fear the loss of human freedom as we all do to fear overpopulation in a world where the leopard will lie down with the lamb, or to fear interminable senility in a world where death shall be no more. The reason for this lies in the recognition of the ultimacy of what is promised, its eschatological character. Hans Walter Wolff effectively summed up the place of Jer. 31:31–34 within the prophetic message as a whole, when, in "Das Thema 'Umkehr' in der alttestamentlichen Prophetie," he explained the place of repentance in the prophets by tracing the metaphor of return. In contrast to what a Christian revivalist heritage might suggest, he documented how "return" does not appear as a demand in the prophets. In the older prophets, e.g. Amos, it appears primarily in the indicative rather than the imperative, stating what did not happen ("You did not return"). When the term does appear in the imperative, as in Jeremiah, it often does so not as a demand, but as an invitation, i.e., motivated by a following promise ("Return, . . . I will . . .). And in Jer. 31:31–34, Wolff sees a bold affirmation of the end of the road of return, i.e., the Lord will give His people return ("I will bring you back"). The point is simply this: The Lord promises to give what He seeks, not in dismal despair, but in the triumph of mercy (ZThK 48, 1951, pp. 129–148). While this appears to me to be a line of exegetical approach inherently equally available to both Jewish and Christian scholars, I recognize that this line is not one usually followed by Jews. I venture to suggest that it may be that Jews perceive this analysis of repentance in the prophets to be reflective of Christian ideas about original sin. Of course, one could bring that concept in by pointing out with old dogmaticians how in creation God made humans able not to sin (*posse non peccare*), but as a result of the Fall they became unable not to sin (*non posse non peccare*), only to hear the promise that in the consummation they will become unable to sin (*non posse peccare*). But I do not feel there is any inherent necessity to make such a connection. No theory of original sin is needed to elaborate the prophetic presentation of the disobedience of God's people. With unanimity, prophets, most especially Jeremiah, Ezekiel, and the Deuteronomistic historian's *"Prophetenaussage"* agree monotonously in the verdict, "They did not listen (obey)."

Now, when one goes on to ask about the setting reflected by Jer. 31:31–34, a variety of possible areas of exploration is opened up. First, one might consider chronological setting, i.e., the examination of the historical background reflected. There should not be much difference between Jews and Christians here; yet sometimes the assignment of this text to an exilic date, because of deuteronomic or deuteronomistic influence (cf. the work of S. Herrmann), does get to be a minor matter of difference. Next, one might think of sociological setting, i.e., how did this prophetic word function? This is basic to form criticism. Here a difference appears in that Jewish writers tend more to think of written literature designed for reading. This is also the pattern of those Christians not decisively influenced by the heritage of form-criticism. Still, there is much commonality here. If it were my assignment to be analyzing Jeremiah for *FOTL,* I'd have to ask about the fantastically violent way in which this contrast preaching dealt with sacred traditions. How could a prophet dare to talk this way as one who stood within these traditions? Comparison reveals that prophets here take on the incredible task of announcing the cancellation of the old as part of their proclamation of the eschatological new. Here is a big difference between Jews and some Christians! Jews and most Christian exegetes will not talk the language of the cancellation of election, preferring to speak of "suspension." It is not hard to see why. Speaking of cancellation could easily reflect some naive view of supercession, i.e., Christianity as the new covenant, and Jews as the former people of God who were rejected by the prophets and are thereby out. I reject any such supercessionism. That is not an issue in exegesis. The issue here is what is the intention of the prophet. With an audience which refused to accept the prophet's message of judgment (spoken of as rejection, doom, and death) because of their faith in God's election promises (exodus-covenant, Zion, and David), the prophet takes the ultimate step. He affirms a future marked by basic discontinuity, one which comes only as life out of death. He does not talk of suspension of covenant, he talks of cancellation. As Hosea actually said, so Jeremiah implies, "I am not your God, and you are not my people." This is, I think, the clear implication of the future tense in the covenant formula in v. 33. Hosea also offers the same sort of promise, "It shall be said to them, 'Sons of the living God.'" This issue has nothing to do with respect for Jews or theories of supercession. It is just the task of exegesis to explore the exact flavor of what was said in its sociological context, here as preaching, but also as tradition-history. No real differences should appear here, but the history of polemic in the past has made it almost impossible for Jews to use this "tainted" terminology, even if within a new context. Finally, one might look at the redactional setting, i.e., the arrangement of passages. Here the focus would be with chapters 30 and 31 and in relation to chapters 32 and 33. Levin's joining of 31:27–30 to 31–34 is a case in point. Here, there are no real differences; in fact Jews are often at home in and ahead of Christian structuralists with their focus on editorial devices. Sometimes rabbinic principles of interpretation have a productive relevance here.

In all these phases of exegesis the basic technique employed is to examine a passage in the light of others. To explore form, one looks at other examples of the same or a similar genre. In literary criticism, one attempts a relative dating and a reconstruction of the sequence of related passages. In examining setting, the chronological setting is explored by means of other passages which provide information on the background in history. To look at sociological setting, one investigates other passages which provide information on the function of similar units within that community. In regard to the redactional setting, one looks by definition at how this passage is linked to others in some kind of logical arrangement. This just reveals that all scientific study is essentially the study of context. But now we must face the question about the extent of the context. Both Jews and Christians are inclined to deal with biblical context, but with a different definition of Bible. This question of the extent of context could be just a matter of how far to look for historical connections, but

I ask you to recall the framework within which exegesis functions. A whole new discipline of "canonical criticism" has grown up as a way of coming systematically to terms with this long-ignored aspect, but the reality has always been there. The issue of the extent of the context becomes then a matter of basic disagreement between Jews and Christians. Sometimes the presence of this factor has been surprising and misunderstood. In S. Boehmer's *Heimkehr und neuer Bund* (p. 79), the discussion of Jer. 31:31–34 concludes by speaking of forgiveness in terms of wrath and grace, with some analogies in this area from the work of the Deuteronomist. Suddenly in the final two-line paragraph, these words appear: "The unity of God's wrath and grace would first be revealed in the cross of Jesus Christ" (my own free translation). What is that remark doing there? I can just imagine an HUC rabbinic student writing in the margin, "Christian bias!"

As I have tried to suggest by introducing this area as a matter of context, there is a logic behind such surprising Christian observations. But this logic is often misunderstood—even more by Christians than by Jews! In the *Biblischer Kommentar* series, the last area treated in the examination of any passage is that of *Ziel,* freely paralleled in the Intention section in *FOTL* volumes. In Jon Levenson's review of Zimmerli's BK volume II on Ezekiel (Because the BK volume on Jeremiah, published in fascicles, is still far from complete, I choose an example from the most closely related book), he says:

> Unlike Zimmerli the text-critic and Zimmerli the redaction-critic, Zimmerli the preacher is quite traditional and quite conservative, surprisingly so. He does not seem to sense any problem in offering a Christian interpretation of a non-Christian book. For example, in applying II Corinthians 5:17 to the vision of the dry bones (Ezek. 37:1–14), he blithely denationalizes Ezekiel's prophecy (p. 266). It is no longer a vision of the miraculous restoration of the *people Israel* after their exile, but a comment on the *individual* who comes into *Christ.* The difference is so glaring that one wonders about the intellectual schizophrenia that allows this kind of preaching to be appended to critical discussion of the text.
>
> *Interpretation* 1984, p. 212

To think the *Ziel* sections are appended preaching is a tragic mistake. Admittedly, the goal of formulating a text's "essential message" (to use the term I employ in teaching exegesis) is to be carried out with a concern for what Germans call *Transparenz,* i.e., a formulation in which the specific historical "accidents" are minimized, so that one can see "through" the text to its on-going point. But this formulation of "the point of the text" is a basic part of the exegetical process. In the instance Levenson refers to, Zimmerli happens to point to the reinterpretation of the hope of Ezekiel 37 that the New Testament provides. This is a matter, however, of tracing further the on-going reinterpretation of God's creative action, which has already begun in Ezekiel in the way the raising of the dry bones is described as taking place in two stages. This reminds the listener of the creation account in Gen. 2, all of which Zimmerli discusses at length. Levenson misunderstands what is going on, because he has different presuppositions about what one might expect from a commentary on a prophet by a Christian writer. And, alas, Levenson is fully justified in that expectation on the basis of many pious stupidities which appear when commentators wax homiletical. In this case, he was misled by a false pre-understanding, and perhaps by a lack of familiarity with the methodological discussions which years ago were published as a preliminary to the BK series. What is essentially involved in the inclusion of the New Testament within the context of an Old Testament passage is the experience-rooted conviction that heuristic value is to be found through this method. This is simply something which has been the historical experience of scholars. The mutual fructification of Old and New Testament form-criticism and redaction criticism is only a most obvious illustration. But then, by definition this exploration of canonical context is one aspect of the exegetical enterprise where we can expect, in view of different canons, to find the sharpest differences, and ones which almost inevitably must be expected to remain. After all, as has been repeatedly affirmed (cf. Zwi Werblowsky, "Tora als Gnade," *Kairos* 15, 1973, pp. 156–162), although it is an inherent part of Christianity that Christians must concern themselves with Judaism because of their roots, there is not any real necessity for Jews to deal with Christianity any more than with any other religion in the world of today. Thus one would not be justified in requiring that Jewish exegetes pay attention to tne New Testament context of passages in the Hebrew Bible. Neither would it be appropriate to forget the context within the faith of the church, out of which the Christian exegete not only comes to, but receives the text of the Old Testament. In the specific case of Jer. 31:31–34, this issue of context is one which arises at every Eucharist, when the words are heard,

"This cup is the new covenant in my blood" (I Cor. 11:25 and Luke 22:20). Here we stand at the very center of Christian worship and life. What is to be found there is not primarily a question of historical context, which belongs solely to the domain of the historian. Here, the historian's preoccupation with how things have come to be the way they are, a descriptive question, is overshadowed by the existential issue of one's own identity, which is a normative matter.

RICHARD S. SARASON

7. *The Interpretation of Jeremiah 31:31–34 in Judaism*

Ἐν ἀηχη ἦν ὁ λὸγος . . .
In the beginning was the Word . . .

John 1:1

That the interpretation of Hebrew Scripture should play such a prominent role historically in the Jewish-Christian encounter is hardly surprising. Both rabbinic Judaism and Christianity are products of the late Hellenistic world which venerated ancient texts for their antiquity, and sacred texts for their authority, displaying considerable ingenuity in the exegesis of each. Both the rabbis and the believers in Christ saw themselves as the true and rightful heirs of ancient Israel, the inheritors of its literature, and the audience addressed by its prophets. Both viewed Scripture as oracular, and ancient prophecy as susceptible to fulfillment in their own lifetimes. Given these shared presuppositions about the importance of Scripture as divine communication and the "wide" parameters of its legitimate meanings, it is easy to understand how Christians, schematizing their own religious experience, could appeal to prophetic texts both to communicate and to validate the Messiahship of Jesus, while rabbinic Jews, proceeding from a different religious experience and unconvinced by the messianic claims for Jesus, could read these same messianic prophecies without christological overtones. Such divergent readings are found in the exegesis of Jeremiah 31:31–34, which Christians early understood as prophetic of their new experience in Christ, and which is the literary source of the term "New Testament" (*b^e^rit ḥadašah;* καινὴ διαθήκη; *novum testamentum*).[1] This paper will survey the interpretation of Jer. 31:31–34 in Judaism from late antiquity through the nineteenth century, and conclude with my own studied observations on the meaning of the text.[2]

Before proceeding, I believe that some general remarks are in order on the function of Scripture and scriptural interpretation in early rabbinic Judaism. The fact that we concentrate here on a text that has been more important for Christianity than for Judaism, and has been one of the many loci of Jewish-Christian polemics, may otherwise skew our perspective on an activity which, in rabbinic Judaism, has its own internal logic. For the rabbis of late antiquity, the Torah—not the Prophets—formed the central core of Scripture, because it contained God's revealed instruction to Israel regulating both social and divine-human intercourse. A life conducted in accordance with the Torah's precepts and a society governed by them conformed to the will of God. Of greater significance for the rabbis themselves, the study of Torah—both Scripture and their own traditions—constituted the religious activity *par excellence* because it brought the human mind into contact with the revealed mind of God. In late antique rabbinic Judaism, Torah is the ultimate mediator between man and God, and the study of Torah the ultimate mode of access to divine power. In this mediating capacity, rabbinic Torah is the precise functional equivalent of Christ in Christianity.[3] Thus the study of Scripture, augmented—and ultimately superseded—by rabbinic traditions, assumed enormous importance in Judaism. Most of the rabbinic scriptural exegesis from late antiquity focuses on the Torah. All of the exegetical compilations excepting the *Pesiqtot* (compilations of exegeses relevant to synagogal lections for holidays and fast days) are redacted around the Torah or those hagiographa that were read in the synagogue (e.g., Lamentations, Song of Songs, Psalms). None are redacted around the prophetic books. Only those ten prophetic lections read in synagogues during the weeks around the Ninth of Ab serve as exegetical foci in the two *Pesiqtot.* Nonetheless, there are scores of exegeses on individual verses from the prophetic literature. Most of these verses are juxtaposed, on the basis of real or perceived verbal similarities, with other scriptural verses, usually from the Torah, in order to shed light on the deeper meaning of each. Messianic prophecies are frequently found at the conclusion of homiletic chapters where they refer to the coming divine vindication of Israel, and serve as a source of comfort in present circumstances.

With this background in mind, we may now turn to the exegesis of Jer. 31:31ff. The evidence from late antiquity differs in two striking respects from its medieval counterpart: first, it is much sparser, and, second, it appears to be completely free of polemical thrust vis à vis Christianity. On the basis of the textual evidence we cannot show that any rabbis were aware of the christological interpretation of this passage and responded to it. Noteworthy, too, is the fact that, in the form in which the materials have been redacted for literary transmission, there is no autonomous or primary exegesis of this passage; its exegesis always proceeds through juxtaposition with other verses which, in their present redactional context, are primary. In other words, the Jeremiah verses always appear in the literature as prooftexts.

The earliest exegetical use of our passage appears in *Sifra*, a compilation to Leviticus of mostly halakhic materials. Edited in the Land of Israel in roughly the third century CE, *Sifra* is probably the earliest midrashic compilation we possess. Here, our passage is juxtaposed with Lev. 26:9 to clarify the meaning of the latter verse—specifically to show that it refers to the messianic future. God's promise in the Torah that "if you follow My laws and faithfully observe My commandments, I will grant peace in the land ... and I will maintain My covenant with you" remains valid, but must have a future referent, since Israel has disobeyed the commandments and suffered the consequences. The promise of Lev. 26 to *maintain* the covenant (*w^e^haqimoti et b^e^riti*) is identified with the making of a "new" covenant in Jeremiah 31:31—"not like the first covenant which you violated, but a new covenant which will never again be broken, as it is written, *See the time is coming—declares the Lord—when I will make a new covenant...*" We shall see further on that several medieval commentators make polemical use of the assertion that the new covenant's "novelty" is simply that it will never again be violated,[4] but I do not detect those overtones here. The focus of this exegetical juxtaposition is rather on the messianic referent of the Leviticus verse.

The eleven other references to our passage appear in documents from the Land of Israel, dating from roughly the fourth or fifth through the ninth or tenth centuries CE.[5] They actually contain only eight independent traditions, five of which share the same motif; the other three are relatively trivial instances of prooftexting that need not detain us here.[6] The five texts at hand[7] relate to Jer. 31:33–34, *"I will put my Torah into their inmost being and inscribe it upon their hearts.... No longer will they need to teach one another...."* For all their diversity, the texts indicate a common rabbinic understanding of these verses as referring to Torah *study*, that rabbinic salvific activity *par excellence*, rather than *observance* of God's Teaching—which is what Jeremiah and the editors of his book had in mind. The shared motif, expressing a quintessentially rabbinic concern, is that in this world scholars are constitutionally inclined to forget the Torah which they have labored so long to learn and memorize; but in the world to come, Torah will be learned (in some versions directly from God) and not forgotten, as it is written, *"I will put my Torah into their inmost being and inscribe it upon their hearts."* I cite two examples to give the flavor of this line of interpretation:

> R. Judan in the name of R. Judah b. Simon and R. Judah and R. Nehemiah joined issue. R. Judah said: When Israel heard the words, *I am the Lord thy God,* the knowledge of the Torah was fixed in their heart and they learnt and forgot not. They came to Moses and said, 'Our master, Moses, do thou become an intermediary between us, as it says, *"Speak thou with us, and we will hear"... now therefore why should we die* (Ex. 20:16; Deut. 5:22). What profit is there in our perishing?' They then became liable to forget what they learnt. They said: Just as Moses, being flesh and blood, is transitory, so his teaching is transitory. Forthwith they came a second time to Moses and said: 'Our master, Moses, would that God might be revealed to us a second time! Would that He would kiss us WITH THE KISSES OF HIS LIPS! Would that He would fix the knowledge of the Torah in our hearts as it was!' He replied to them: 'This cannot be now, but it will be in the days to come,' as it says, *I will put My law in their inward parts and in their heart will I write it* (Jer. 31:33). R. Nehemiah said: When Israel heard the command *'Thou shalt not have'*, the Evil Inclination was plucked from their heart. They came to Moses and said to him: 'Our master Moses, become thou an intermediary between us, as it says, *"Speak thou with us and we shall hear ... now therefore why should we die."* What profit is there in our perishing? Straightway the Evil Inclination returned to its place. They returned to Moses and said to him, 'Moses, would that God would reveal Himself to us a second time. Would that He would kiss us WITH THE KISSES OF HIS MOUTH! He replied to them: 'This cannot be now, but in time to come it will be, as it says, *And I will take away the stony heart out of your flesh*' (Exek. 36:26).

Song of Songs Rabba, 1.2.4,
to Song 1:2 [c. fourth–fifth c. CE];
trans. Maurice Simon, ed. Soncino: 1939.

> I SAID IN MY HEART: COME NOW, I WILL TRY YOU WITH MIRTH (Eccles. 2:1). R. Phinehas and R. Hezekiah in the name of R. Simon b. Zabdi commented on this. R. Phinehas said: [The text can be read as] *anassekah*

(I will try thee) and *anuskah* (I will flee thee). I will make a test with words of Torah and I will make a test with words of heresy; I will flee from words of heresy to words of Torah. AND ENJOY PLEASURE: i.e. the pleasure of Torah. AND, BEHOLD, THIS ALSO WAS VANITY! The verse should have stated nothing else than 'And, behold, this also was *pleasure*'; but it declares, AND, BEHOLD, THIS ALSO WAS VANITY! R. Hezekiah said in the name of R. Simon b. Zabdi: All the Torah which you learn in this world is 'vanity' in comparison with Torah [which will be learnt] in the World to Come; because in this world a man learns Torah and forgets it, but with reference to the World to Come what is written there? *I will put My law in their inward parts* (Jer. 31:33).

Ecclesiastes Rabba, 2.1,
to Eccles. 2:1 [c. eighth–ninth c. CE];
trans. A. Cohen, ed. Soncino: 1939

Two points are noteworthy about these exegeses. First, they are pristine examples of what rabbinic exegesis of these verses looks like without any reference to Christian interpretation—a phenomenon which, as we shall see, no longer exists in the medieval literature. Second, and more subtly, the rabbis here employ exactly the same kind of "wide" exegetical parameters as does the author of Hebrews in offering a christological interpretation of the text. This, too, changes in medieval exegesis, as rabbinic Jews, confronted on the one hand with christological interpretations (Christian "wide" midrash) and on the other with Karaite attacks on rabbinic "wide" midrash, will attempt to narrow the range of legitimate textual meanings to the *p^{e}shat*, the "plain sense" of Scripture.[8]

We turn now to the medieval evidence. Jewish interpretations of Jer. 31:31ff. in the medieval period are found in two literary genres: 1) polemical literature, where the christological interpretation of this passage is directly addressed and refuted,[9] and 2) exegetical literature, i.e., verse-by-verse commentaries on the Book of Jeremiah among the other scriptural books, where the christological interpretation may be addressed directly, indirectly, or ignored. We shall deal with these two genres in turn, beginning with the polemical literature.

The earliest extant acknowledgment and refutation of christological interpretation of Jer. 31:31 is found in Saadia's *Book of Doctrines and Beliefs (Kitāb al-'Amānāt wa'l-I'tikādāt)*, written in Babylonia in 933 CE. Saadia ibn Yussif al-Fayyumi (882–942) was a spirited polemicist for the rabbanite position against Karaism, Islam, Zoroastrianism, Christianity, and other philosophical and religious positions then current in his surroundings. In this context, he was the first major rabbanite grammarian and author of a p^e*shat*-commentary (in Arabic) on the Torah. He thus stands at the head of both literary streams that we shall be following. In the third treatise of the *Kitāb*, "Concerning Command and Prohibition," Saadia deals with the rational necessity for revelation, and polemicizes against both Moslem and Christian claims that the Mosaic Law has been abrogated. He notes three scriptural verses that have been cited by "some of the proponents of the theory of abrogation," and counters their interpretations. The last of these verses is Jer. 31:31.[10] Saadia refutes his opponents by calling their attention to the context of this verse. He writes:

> "Why don't you look at what follows this verse, where it is explicitly stated that this new covenant that was mentioned before is the Torah itself?" Thus, Scripture says, *But this is the covenant I will make . . . I will put my Torah in their inmost parts . . . (31:33). It would only be different from the first covenant in this respect: that it would not be broken this time as it was the first time, as Scripture says, Forasmuch as they broke my covenant . . .* (31:32).
>
> (Trans. S. Rosenblatt, p. 167)

All of the subsequent European polemical literature which deals with this passage makes exactly the same point: that the Torah of Moses is not abrogated at the end of days of which Jeremiah speaks. Rather the new covenant refers to and renews the Torah of Moses, simply altering the manner of its transmission and observance by Israel: God's Torah will be totally internalized, so that Israel will never again break the covenant by violating God's commandments. Some of the European polemicists also appeal explicitly to the context of verse 31 for its interpretation, as does Saadia.[11]

A review of the European Jewish polemical literature for our purposes is best done schematically. First, some words of background. The bulk of this literature hails from Spain and Southern France during and after the period of the Reconquista, but some tracts were written in Italy and the Rhineland as well. A notable sixteenth-century tract was written in Lituania by a Karaite, Isaac of Troki, and gained considerable popularity among rabbanites. Some of this literature remains in manuscript; we deal here only with published materials.[12] The literature is cast into three basic genres: 1) literary disputations between Jewish and Christian sages, some based on actual public disputations or conversations (notably Nahmanides' account of his disputation in July 1263, with Fra Paulo Christiani), some fictive;[13] 2) topical treatises, in which specific claims of Christianity are taken up and refuted;[14] 3) collocations of biblical texts, book by book, with refutations of their christological interpretations.[15] This latter genre also includes systematic attacks on New Testament passages. Jer. 31:31ff. is not dealt with in every polemical text;[16] it is not as ubiquitously treated as, e.g., some of the classic messianic prooftexts in Isaiah. Still, it appears by my count in fifteen tracts—a not inconsiderable number—and figures prominently in every discussion of the eternity vs. abrogation of the Torah in the messianic age, where it constitutes perhaps the classic Christian prooftext on the Christian side, and is rebutted in stock fashion on the Jewish side. The appended chart catalogues the elements of this rebuttal. We shall point out here some of the more interesting variations. Two aspects of the passage are routinely addressed: the meaning of the "new covenant" in v. 31ff. and the import of the heightened knowledge of God in v. 34 as a sign of the onset of the messianic age. We shall deal with each of these in turn.

(1) The New Covenant. All of our authors who deal with this part of the passage understand the Christian interpretation as claiming not merely that the new covenant foretold by Jeremiah entails the abrogation of the Mosaic Torah, but also that the Gospel of Jesus which is to be "inscribed on their hearts" constitutes a *new Torah.*[17] To this they reply univocally that the Torah of Moses will never be abrogated in the messianic age[18] and that no new Torah will ever be given. Azriel Petaḥia b. Moshe Alatino, in his dispute with Don Alfonso Caracciola, asserts that Jeremiah could not possibly contradict what Moses and the other prophets maintain: that the Torah is eternal. Isaac of Troki painstakingly points out, e.g., that the terms "covenant" and "Torah" are not synonymous, that Scripture speaks of many covenants made by God with individuals (Phineas, the patriarchs), that did not entail new, individual Torahs. Similarly here, Jeremiah speaks of a new covenant, not a new Torah. The Torah of v. 33 is that same Mosaic Torah, just differently transmitted and more perfectly observed. What is novel about the new covenant is rather to be learned from vv. 32–34: (a) unlike the former covenant, which was broken by the Israelites' disobedience, this one will never be broken (Saadia, Jacob b. Reuben, et al.) since (b) this time the Mosaic Torah will be inscribed on people's hearts, so that it will never again be forgotten

(*Niṣ. Vet.,* Yair b. Shabtai, Troki) or disobeyed (Durans). Indeed, asserts Isaac b. Joseph Israeli, all Israel will be totally righteous, performing God's will wholeheartedly. He also maintains that Jeremiah here merely repeats the covenant promises of Leviticus and Deuteronomy, adding nothing. Simeon b. Ṣemaḥ Duran even contends that the expression "new covenant" is misleading. The covenant is "new" only to the extent that it has not been fully actualized in the past; but *in potentia* it is the same covenant. Jacob b. Reuben also speaks of the "renewal" of the covenant and the bonds of love between God and Israel.

Several of our authors take this occasion to go on the offensive against their Christian adversaries. Jacob b. Reuben, Moses Ha-Kohen, and the anonymous compiler of *Niṣṣaḥon Vetus* accuse the Christians of self-contradiction. How can they maintain that Jeremiah fortells a new Torah given by Jesus when Jesus himself, according to Matthew 5:17–19, claims "I have come not to destroy the Torah of Moses or the words of the prophets, but to fulfill them. Heaven and earth shall pass, but not a thing shall pass from the words of Moses"? These disputants thus appeal to the literary remains in the Gospels of what was indeed a matter of heated debate in the early Church. *Niṣ. Vet.* goes on to ask why, if the new covenant is to be the Gospel of Jesus, Jeremiah does not explicitly say so here; why Israel and Judah are mentioned here, rather than all the nations (so also Simeon b. Ṣemaḥ Duran). Profiat Duran wants to know how "the uncircumcized" can see themselves addressed in these verses, when their forefathers had not been brought by God out of Egypt. Here, of course, our authors enter the *Verus Israel* debate. Finally, both Profiat Duran and, after him, Simeon b. Ṣemaḥ Duran accuse Paul (whom they view as the author of Hebrews) and Jerome of having misconstrued the force of the verb *natati* in v. 33 (*natati et torati b^{e}qirbam*). For Duran, the use of the perfect tense here indicates that the Torah which in the messianic age "I will put in their inmost parts" is the same Torah "which I *gave* them" in the past. The artificiality of this line of argumentation is patent, but fairly common in medieval polemics on all sides.

(2) Increased knowledge of the Lord (v. 34) as one of the signs of the messianic age. Eight of our authors, beginning with Nahmanides in his disputation with Paulo Christiani, acknowledge that in the days of the Messiah both knowledge of God and the piety resulting therefrom will increase. But, looking at the world around them, they see no evidence that the messianic age has arrived.[19] Nahmanides writes, "Since the days of Jesus up to the present, the whole world has been full of violence and

rapine, the Christians more than other peoples being shedders of blood and revealers of indecencies" (Rankin, p. 192). In this context Joseph Official takes a nasty swipe at the Dominican Predicant friars. "How," he asks, "can Christians maintain that they all know the Lord when every day we see those baying hounds barking at them and dispensing *poenitentia*?" Solomon de' Rossi, on the other hand, poignantly explains that knowledge of the Lord will increase among the gentiles in the messianic age because they will all be witness to God's miraculous redemption of Israel from their midst—a redemption made more miraculous by contrast with Israel's despised and persecuted lot in exile.

The polemical literature thus reveals a stock set of responses to christological exegesis of Jer. 31:31ff., with some interesting variations among them. Similar conclusions will follow from a review of the exegetical literature, in which, as Erwin I. J. Rosenthal reminds us, polemics play an integral part.[20] As was the case in late antiquity, more exegetical attention is focused subsequently on the Torah than any other part of Scripture, but there are a good number of commentaries on other books as well, Jeremiah among them. Out of nine commentaries on the Book of Jeremiah which deal with our passage,[21] three confine themselves to grammatical comments alone,[22] while the other six repeat with variations themes that we have already seen in the polemical literature. There is additonal relevant material in the Torah commentaries of Nahmanides and Rashi, though no word at all on our pericope in Rashi's commentary on Jeremiah 31.

In his commentary to Lev. 26:9, Rashi cites verbatim the *Sifra* passage we discussed earlier. Since Rashi routinely cites or paraphrases midrashic material that he deems relevant, it is not clear whether this comment should be viewed as having polemical intent or overtones. On the other hand, Rashi openly polemicizes against christological interpretations in his commentary on Psalms.

Most interesting are the remarks of Nahmanides in his comment on Deuteronomy 30:6, God's promise to "circumcise the hearts" of the Israelites at the time of their future redemption. Nahmanides insightfully juxtaposes this verse with our Jeremiah passage and with Ezekiel 36:26, the "new heart and new spirit" which God will put within the Israelites at that time, thereby causing them to follow His laws. All three passages, he says, mean the same thing: in the messianic future, man's nature will be restored to its pristine state before the sin of Adam. The evil impulse, i.e., the impulse to rebel against God's will, will be abolished. Man will *naturally* desire to do what is right, and consequently will not need to be exhorted, instructed, or legislated to do so. At issue, then, in these passages is the problematic nature of man's will. Nahmanides' approach is very much in line with what I shall propose below is the actual meaning of our passage.

Of the six commentators who deal directly with Jer. 31:31ff., the three from Spain and southern France are most overtly polemical. David Kimḥi's commentaries are filled with anti-christological polemics,[23] and our passage is no exception. He explicitly denies there will ever be a new Torah or an abrogation of the Mosaic Torah, appealing to Malachi's final eschatological words (to which the Gospels, of course, also appeal). The novelty of the new covenant is, again, to be explained from context, viz., that, unlike the first one, this one will be permanent; it will never be broken, because the Torah will be inscribed on people's hearts, so that it cannot be forgotten. Kimḥi here is very much in line with the polemical literature. Joseph Naḥmias appeals to a well-known midrash (*Sifre, Wa'etḥanan* 33) to explain why the covenant is called "new," since it only refers to the Mosaic Torah. That Torah, he says, is eternally new, since Israel should relate to the Torah each day as if they had just received it *hayom*—today. For Naḥmias, too, context proves that the "novelty" lies simply in the perfect observance of the Mosaic Torah, and thereby refutes the Christian claims "which are without substance." Don Isaac Abravanel notes that "the enemies of the Lord and the heretics have gone wide of the mark [in interpreting these verses] and have polemicized much against us." There will never be a new Torah, he maintains; rather the new covenant refers to the new *inclination* to observe the Mosaic Torah which God will implant within the people in the messianic age. Here, Abravanel adds an arresting nuance: the people will be so awestruck by the miracles which God will perform before their eyes at the end of time that the evil impulse will be driven out of them, and they will willingly submit to God's rule.

Samuele Davide Luzzatto's remarks are also polemical. He refers his readers to the rebuttals of Kimḥi and Abravanel, adding that Jeremiah's prophecy has not yet been fulfilled, since humankind is still far from moral perfection: the Torah is not yet inscribed upon our hearts. He also juxtaposes our passage with Deut. 30:6 and with Jer. 32:37–41, God's promise to give the people "a single heart and a single nature to revere Me for all time" and to make "an everlasting covenant with them that I will not turn away from them . . .; and I will put into their hearts reverence for Me, so that they do not turn away from Me." I will maintain below that this passage is indeed identical in meaning to our own.

Polemical intent is less clear in the two commentaries from Eastern Europe, those of David Altschuler and Meir Loeb Malbim. Altschuler notes that the nature of the covenant will be new: it will not be broken by *either* party. God will remain faithful to the Israelites to save and protect them; at the same time, the Israelistes will remain faithful to God, believing in Him and observing His commandments. Altschuler holds that the *crux interpretatem* in v. 32, *w'anokhi ba'alti bam,* means that even when the Israelites vioalted God's covenant, God nonetheless remained faithful to them, saving them from their enemies. He also holds that God's promise in the future to "put my Torah in their inmost parts" means that God will incline the Israelites' hearts to observe His Torah. There is probably an implicit polemic here. Finally, Malbim gives a rather unique rationale for the necessity of a new covenant in the future. The old covenant was conditional upon the Israelites' not sinning. But in the messianic age they will be morally perfect and naturally inclined to observe God's laws. Since they will be incapable of sinning, a new kind of covenant will be necessary: a new covenant for a new human nature. Here there is no explicit polemical thrust and it is unclear whether one is intended.

This completes our survey of the exegetical literature, where we note a wider range of variation than in the polemical literature, as we could expect from the different nature of the two genres. Having presented a rather thorough overview of the interpretation of Jer. 31:31ff. in Jewish tradition, I now turn to my own understanding of the passage.

I approach this passage both as a Jew and a critically-trained humanistic scholar of religion, who wants to know what the text conveyed in its original cultural context, while recognizing that, in other contexts, it has come to bear other meanings. I thus consciously limit myself to a "narrow" contextual approach to the text. The relevant contexts are literary (the Book of Jeremiah as finally redacted, the biblical literature as a whole), historical (the periods of Jeremiah and of the redactors of the book that bears his name), and cultural (the culture of ancient Israel in its Near Eastern setting in the sixth century BCE). Relevant indicators of meaning in the text are linguistic, stylistic, and rhetorical.

Our passage forms one member in a series of prophecies of redemption that comprise chapters 30–33. The editor of the book, through his narrative superscriptions at the beginning of chapters 29, 32, and 33, assigns these prophecies to the period after the exile of Jehoiachin, when the final destruction of Jerusalem is imminent. Jerusalem must be destroyed and its disobedient inhabitants punished, asserts the prophet. But the story does not end there. God still loves His people; after seventy years, long enough for the offending generation to die out "in the wilderness," He will redeem them and restore them to Zion. At that time God will initiate a new chapter in the history of His relationship with His people by making a new covenant with them. This is what our passage, viewed in context, promises. In the past, according to Jeremiah, the problem has been the people's disobedience: they have broken the covenant by violating God's Torah—His revealed Teaching and Instruction. Jeremiah has had much to say about man's "evil heart," i.e., the human proclivity to rebel against God: "Most devious is the heart; it is perverse—who can fathom it?" (17:9). The problem of man's resistance to God is a major theme—perhaps *the* major theme—in biblical anthropology (Nahmanides wisely links this passage with the story of Adam in Genesis). I believe this problem is also the major concern of our passage, in which it is ultimately solved by God's radical intervention. Our passage must be juxtaposed with Jeremiah's previous warnings, e.g., 11:6–8:

> Hear the terms of the covenant, and perform them. For I have repeatedly and persistently warned your fathers from the time I brought them out of Egypt to this day, saying, Obey my commands. But they would not listen or give ear; they all followed the willfulness of their evil hearts. So I have applied to them all the terms of this covenant, because they did not do what I commanded them to do.

Our passage recalls this situation and rectifies it. The new covenant will be different; it will not be broken, because it cannot be broken. God's Torah, that is, His commandments and requirements for proper human behavior (not as fully ramified in the time of Jeremiah as subsequently in Jewish tradition) this time will not be given externally through a mediator or in writing on stone tablets, as was done at Sinai, but will be implanted directly by God into the human heart, as the seat of the mind and will. This, of course, is a metaphor for the alteration of human nature so as to conform automatically with God's will; the possibility of disobedience thereby ceases to exist. That is why people will no longer need to be instructed or exhorted to know, i.e., to heed, God; this will literally become "second nature." Our passage should be juxtaposed with 24:6–7, and 32:38–40; with Ezekiel 11:29–20 and 36:26–28; and with Deut. 30:6. All these passages use similar metaphors to convey the same idea: that God will intervene to alter human nature and thus assure a happy future.

Jeremiah, in light of the contemporary catastrophe, apparently despairs of the people's ability to change themselves ("to repent"; see, by contrast, 24:6–7), and requires God to do it for them in a radical fashion. Seen in this light, the prophecy sems bleak indeed, fraught with a profound pessimism about human nature. Seen from another perspective, however, at the time of the people's greatest despondency, Jeremiah holds out a beacon of hope: he assures them that God still loves them so much as to intervene to rectify the situation radically and permanently.[24] He will do for them what heretofore they have not been able to do for themselves: He will grant them the gift of obedience.[25] Thus the prophecy is ultimately hopeful in the extreme.

In light of this analysis, the early christological interpretation of our passage in Hebrews is, of course, tendentious. But we can appreciate how this tendentious interpretation was generated in light of the early Christians' religious experiences and the concerns which they brought to the text. They, too, found human nature problematic and looked to radical divine intervention for salvation; their existential mood thus corresponds to one aspect of the passage. They deemed the experience of Christ to effect a radical change in an individual's inner nature. Thus it was not straining too much to see their own experiences reflected in this text. But they also brought with them their troublesome relationship to the Mosaic Torah which was anachronistically read into the text: by "Torah" Jeremiah "must have meant" the spiritual Gospel of Christ, for that is what *we* mean by it.

On the other side, the late antique rabbinic interpretations of our passage, which stress the primacy of Torah study and its perfection in the messianic age, are no less tendentious. The rabbis, too, see their own concerns reflected in Scripture. More subtly, the medieval Jewish rebuttals of christology in our passage are also tendentious. Though they approach more closely the text's original meaning as I understand it, they are compelled to deal with an issue that is simply not there—the abrogation of the Mosiac Torah—and thereby read into the text their own (and the early Christians') conception of Torah, which is far more ramified than was Jeremiah's.

How then, in conclusion, are we to evaluate the results of our study? What constitutes a religious tradition over time is, in large measure, its exegetical ingenuity in thoroughly interweaving new experiences with inherited values and other authoritative sources of the religious community's identity.[26] In this process of interweaving, both the experiences and the sources are modified. Although as self-conscious, critical scholars we recognize the tendentiousness of both Christian and rabbinic "midrash," we must acknowledge that these "midrashim" are frequently constitutive of the identities of these two religious traditions, embodying their basic values. Thus we cannot reasonably request or expect each other to abandon them. We can, I believe, encourage in each other that self-conscious awareness of our own exegetical acts which discourages us from absolutizing them to the detriment of others.

I began this paper by citing the Fourth Gospel. I close by paraphrasing Michel Foucault: There are no "texts"; there are only interpretations.[27]

Notes

1. Hebrews 8:6–13, 10:15–18; cf. also 9:15, 12:24; II Cor. 3:5–14; I Cor. 11:25; Lk. 22:20. See also Justin, *Dialogue with Trypho,* ch. 11. For later authors, see David Berger, *The Jewish-Christian Debate in the High Middle Ages* (Philadelphia: 1979), p. 271, note 20.

2. There is, additionally, a discrepancy between Jewish and Christian tradition in the versification of Jeremiah 31. In the Masoretic text (MT), our materials comprise 31:30–33, since the chapter begins at *koh 'amar 'adonai maṣa' ḥen bamidbar.* The Vulgate and other Christian Bibles begin the chapter one verse earlier, *ba'et hahi' n^{e}'um 'adonai,* which is MT 30:25. This verse in any case can be construed independently of the materials which precede and follow it. The reason for the discrepancy in versification is not clear. The earliest extant Hebrew codex (Leningrad B 19 A, 10th c. CE), which antedates versification, begins a new paragraph with *koh 'amar 'adonai,* while *ba'et hahi'* concludes the preceding paragraph. (The relevant folio of the Aleppo codex is missing.) The Septuagint, on the other hand, has a different ordering of chapters in Jeremiah; ours is chapter 38. The chapter's versification, however, agrees with the Vulgate. I am grateful to my colleague, Prof. David Weisberg, for sharing with me his knowledge of, and insights into, the Masorah.

3. Cf., e.g., Jacob Neusner, *Between Time and Eternity: The Essentials of Judaism* (Encino, CA: 1975), pp. 7–15.

4. Cf. Kimhi and, possibly, Rashi. See also A.3 on the appended chart.

5. *Pesiqta deRab Kahana* and *Song of Songs Rabba* (two references each) are generally dated to the fourth or fifth centuries CE; the *Tanḥuma* literature (four references comprising three independent traditions, of which two equal *Pesiqta deRab Kahana*), *Ecclesiastes Rabba* (one reference), *Eliahu Rabba* (one reference), and *Kallah Rabba* (one reference; Babylonian) are usually dated

between the seventh and tenth centuries CE, following the Arab conquest of the Land of Israel in 640 CE. There are two further references in a Genizah manuscript published under the title *Midrash Ḥadash* by Jacob Mann, *The Bible As Read and Preached in the Old Synagogue*, I (Cincinnati: 1940), and a single reference in *Midrash HaGadol* to Deuteronomy, a thirteenth-century Yemenite work. See Aaron Hyman, *Torah HaKetuvah wehaMesurah,* 2nd ed. (Tel Aviv: 1979), II, p. 214. Hyman's reference there to *Pesiqta Rabbati* is incorrect. The Warsaw edition of that work does indeed refer to Jer. 31:32 at the end of chapter 31, but the citation is wrong; the actual verse is Jer. 3:13 (correctly cited in the Friedmann Vienna edition). Hyman's references to the *Kuzari* of Judah Halevi are also misleading. Jer. 31:31–34 is nowhere cited in that work: the references are rather to Judah ibn Shmuel's footnotes in his edition of the *Kuzari.*

6. (1) *Pespiqta deRab Kahana,* Pisqa 11 (ed. Buber, fol. 98b), *Tanḥuma, R'ey,* section 14 (ed. Warsaw, fol. 109a), *Tanḥuma* ed. Buber, *R'ey,* section 12 (fol. 12b): *I will put my Torah into their inmost being* explains Ps. 40:9, *Your Torah is in my inmost parts.* (2) *Eliahu Rabba,* Ch. 18 (ed. Friedmann, p. 105): "Were it not for Israel and words of Torah, heaven and earth could not endure"—proved by Jer. 33:25, *As surely as I have established my covenant with day and night—the laws of heaven and earth—so I will never reject the offspring of Jacob,* juxtaposed with 31:33, *Such is the covenant . . . I will put my Torah into their inmost being.* (3) *Kallah Rabba* 3:21 (ed. Higger, pp. 243–45): Jer. 31:31–32 cited in support of Akiva's contention that the generation which rebelled against Moses in the wilderness has no share in the World To Come until God, in the messianic age, renews the covenant with Israel and Judah.

The two references in Mann's Genizah text are more interesting. The first (Hebrew section, p. 210) is a formulary peroration to a "homily" dealing with false oaths: "But in the World To Come all Israel will act with reverence for the Holy One, praised be He, and will know (i.e., acknowledge) His grandeur, as it is written, *No longer will they need to teach one another . . .*" The second (Hebrew section, p. 230) is part of a formulary exegetical litany which Mann associates with the scriptural lection for the seventh day of Pesaḥ: "At the first redemption . . . ; at the future (or second) redemption . . ." Our line reads, "At the first redemption [God] revealed [His Torah] with words inscribed upon stone tablets, but in the future *I will inscribe it upon their hearts.* This contrast is indeed what the prophet had in mind.

A passage in the thirteenth-century Yemenite compilation *Midrash HaGadol,* while later, is also relevant. Here Jer. 31:31 is juxtaposed with Deut. 29:11, [*You stand this day, all of you, before the Lord your God . . .*] *to enter into the covenant of the Lord your God, which the Lord your God is concluding with you this day.* "Why does Scripture repeat *this day*? To inform you that if you observe this covenant, you will merit that [messianic] *day* about which it is written, *On that day I will make a new covenant . . .*"; i.e., observance of the Torah hastens the coming of the messianic time and earns one a place in the World To Come—a standard rabbinic notion.

7. *Pesiqta deRab Kahana,* Pisqa 12 (ed. Buber, fol. 107a) [= *Tanḥuma,*

ed. Buber, *Yitro,* section 13 (fol. 38b), with slight variations]; *Tanḥuma, 'Ekeb,* section 11 (ed. Warsaw, fol. 105b); *Song of Songs Rabba,* 1.2.4 (ed. Romm, fol. 4b), 8.12 (ed. Romm, fol. 41b); *Ecclesiastes Rabba* 2:1 (ed. Romm, fol. 6b).

8. Cf. on this point the astute observations of Erwin I. J. Rosenthal, "Anti-Christian Polemic in Medieval Bible Commentaries," *Journal of Jewish Studies* 11 (1960), pp. 117–19, especially the following: "It is [not] often realized . . . that the retreat of the *derash*—it could not be given up since Judaism cannot ever dispense with it—and the consequent stress on the *peshaṭ* was directly caused and made inevitable by the Christians' attack and their attempt at converting the Jews" (p. 117). Rosenthal's statement fails, I believe, to give sufficient weight to other factors, such as the rabbanite-Karaite controversy, which had the same effect, but his general thrust is surely correct.

9. I am grateful to my colleague, Prof. Michael Signer, for directing my attention to the polemical literature when this study was in an embryonic stage.

10. The others are Deut. 33:2 and Obadiah 1:1.

11. Joseph Official, Isaac of Troki; somewhat more implicitly, *Niṣṣaḥon Vetus,* Solomon de' Rossi. All of the other treatments of this verse make implicit reference to context. On the argument from context as a favored Jewish technique for refutation of christological interpretations of single verses, see Berger, pp. 11–12.

12. For an exhaustive bibliography through 1961, see Judah Rosenthal, *"Sifrut haWikuaḥ ha'Anti-noṣrit 'ad sof haMe'ah haShmoneh-'esreh," 'Areshet,* 2 (1960), pp. 130–179, and the supplement in vol. 3 (1961), pp. 433–439. Highlights of this bibliography are described in English in Salo W. Baron, *A Social and Religious History of the Jews,* IX (New York: 1965), pp. 293–297 (note 7), supplemented by Daniel J. Lasker, *Jewish Philosophical Polemics Against Christianity in the Middle Ages* (New York: 1977), pp. 13–22, and Berger, pp. 389–401.

13. Also in this category among the texts we consider here are: Jacob B. Reuben, *Milḥamot 'Adonai*; Isaac b. Joseph Israeli, "Reply to Abner of Burgos"; Yair b. Shabtai, *Ḥereb Pifiyot*; and Azriel Petaḥia b. Moses Alatino, disputation with Don Alfonso Caracciolo.

14. Among our texts: Meir b. Simeon, *Milḥemet Miṣwah*; Solomon b. Moses de' Rosi, *'Edut'Adonai Ne'emanah*; Isaac b. Moses Efodi (Profiat Duran), *Klimat HaGoyim*; Joshua Lorki, *Nusaḥ Haktab* (Letter to Paul de Santa Maria); Ḥasdai Crescas, *Bittul 'Iqaré HaGoyim*; Simeon b. Ṣemaḥ Duran, *Qeshet uMagen*; Isaac b. Abraham of Troki, *Ḥizzuq 'Emunah.* This genre occasionally makes reference to discussions with Christian sages. Both of these genres additionally employ prooftexting.

15. Among our texts: Joseph Official, *Sefer Yosef HaMeqanneh*; the anonymous *Sefer Niṣṣaḥon Vetus*; Moses HaKohen of Tordesillas, *Sefer 'Ezer Ha'emunah.*

16. It is surprising that our passage does not appear at all in, e.g., Yom Tob

Lippmann Muelhausen's *Sefer HaNiṣṣaḥon* (Germany, c. 1410), since this work, too, is a collocation of biblical texts, book by book. Nor does it appear in the fifteenth-century collocation of Benjamin b. Moses of Rome, *Teshubot HaMinim* (in *Qobeṣ 'al yad* 15 [1889]).

17. Justin, *Dialogue with Trypho,* ch. 11, does in fact refer to the Gospel as a "new Torah," but this characterization is not universal in Christian writings or polemics. Cf., e.g., A. Lukyn Williams' response to Isaac of Troki's tract, in *A Manual of Christian Evidences for Jewish People,* I (London: 1919), pp. 180–184, especially p. 181.

18. Outside of the polemical context, the nature and continued validity of rabbinic Torah in the messianic age in fact recurs as a structural problem throughout the history of Judaism in periods of active messianism. The classic analysis of this endemic tension is Gershom Scholem's 1968 essay, "The Crisis of Tradition in Jewish Messianism," reprinted in Scholem, *The Messianic Idea in Judaism and Other Essays on Jewish Spirituality* (New York: 1971), pp. 49–77. See also W. D. Davies, *Torah in the Messianic Age* (Philadelphia: 1952). For an astute fictional portrayal of this problem, see Isaac Bashevis Singer's novella, *Satan in Goray.*

19. Similar observations, of course, early on gave birth in Christianity to the hope for Jesus' Second Coming.

20. See E. I. J. Rosenthal, *loc. cit.,* p. 115.

21. The published commentary on Jeremiah of Meir b. Isaac Arama (c. 1460–1545) ends at chapter 30.

22. Most deal with the meaning of the expression *ba'alti b-* in v. 32. The *crux interpretatem* here also is reflected in the versions.

23. On Kimḥi as a polemicist, see Frank Talmage, "R. David Kimḥi As Polemicist," in *Hebrew Union College Annual* 38 (1967), pp. 213–235, and *David Kimḥi: The Man and the Commentaries* (Cambridge, MA: 1975), *passim.*

24. Cf. the careful analysis of Jeremiah Unterman, *The Relationship of Repentance to Redemption in Jeremiah* (unpublished doctoral dissertation, University of California at Berkeley: 1983), ch. 3; especially pp. 117–128.

25. Prof. Ronald Hals, in his Bronstein Colloquiun paper, refers to God's "promise of the gift of obedience," i.e., "God promises to give what he seeks."

26. See Jonathan Z. Smith, "Sacred Persistence: Toward a Redescription of Canon," in *Imagining Religion: From Babylon to Jonestown* (Chicago: 1982), pp. 36–52; Edward Shils, "Tradition," in *Comparative Studies in Society and History* 13, 2 (April 1971), pp. 122–159, and *Tradition* (Chicago: 1981).

27. See Foucault, "Nietzsche, Freud, Marx," in *Nietzsche,* Cahiers de Royaumart, Philosophie, 6 (Paris: 1967), p. 189: "Il n'y a rien d'absolument premier à interpréter, car au fond, tout est déjà interprétation, chaque signe est en lui-même non pas la chose qui s'offre à l'interprétation, mais interprétation d'autres signes. Il n'y a jamais . . un *interpretandum* qui ne soit déjà *interpretans* . . ."

Appendix A

Themes and Variations in the Medieval Jewish Polemical Literature on Jeremiah 31:31–34. A Synoptic Chart

Themes: / Sources: (full references follow)	① Saadia	② Joseph b. Reuben	③ Meir b. Simeon	④ Moses b. Nahman	⑤ Joseph Official	⑥ Nissahon Vetus	⑦ Solomon b. Moses de' Rossi	⑧ Isaac b. Joseph Israeli	⑩ Profiat Duran	⑪ Hasdai Crescas	⑫ Joshua Lorki	⑬ Simeon b. Semah Durah	⑭ Yair b Shabtai da Corregio	⑮ Isaac of Troki	⑯ Azriel Petahia b Moses Alatino
A. On Jer. 31:31 ff (the new covenant)	√	√	—	—	√	√	√	√	√	—	—	√	√	√	√
1) no new Torah	√	√	—	—	√	√	√	√	√	√	—	√	√	√	√
—covenant is not identical with Torah	—	—	—	—	—	—	—	√	—	—	—	—	—	√	—
—eternity of Torah	—	—	—	—	—	√	√	√	√	√	—	√	√	√	√
—upheld by both Moses and prophets	—	—	—	—	—	—	—	√	—	—	—	—	√	—	—
—Jeremiah says same thing as Deut., Lev.	—	—	—	—	—	—	—	√	—	—	—	—	—	—	—
2) new covenant = *renewal* of covenant	—	√	—	—	—	—	—	√	—	—	—	√	√	—	—
3) novelty of covenant:															
—won't be broken this time	√	√	—	—	—	—	—	—	√	—	—	√	√	√	—
—won't be forgotten (Torah)	—	—	—	—	—	√	—	—	—	—	—	—	√	√	—
—Israel will be totally righteous	—	—	—	—	—	—	—	√	—	—	—	—	—	—	—

4) meaning of new covenant to be determined from context (explicit statement)	√	—	—	—	√	—	—	—	—	—	—	—	—	—	—
5) attacks on Christian position:	—	√	—	—	—	√	—	—	√	—	—	—	—	—	—
—"you contradict yourselves" (vs. Mtt. 5:17–19)	—	√	—	—	—	√	—	—	—	—	—	—	—	—	—
—"Jeremiah should have stated explicitly that new covenant was Gospel of Jesus"	—	—	—	—	—	√	—	—	—	—	—	—	—	—	—
—if the new covenant is directed to all mankind, why does Jeremiah mention Israel and Judah?	—	—	—	—	—	√	—	—	—	—	—	—	—	—	—
—Jeremiah addresses Israel; the Gentiles are not Israel	—	—	—	—	—	—	—	—	√	—	—	√	—	—	—
—their ancestors were not in Egypt	—	—	—	—	—	—	—	—	√	—	—	—	—	—	—
—Paul and Jerome miscontrue the text	—	—	—	—	—	—	—	—	√	—	—	√	—	—	—
B. On Jer. 31:34 (increase of knowledge)	—	—	√	√	√	—	√	—	—	√	√	—	√	√	—
1) signs of Messiah: hasn't happened yet	—	—	√	√	√	—	√	—	—	√	√	—	√	√	—
—Predicant friars still preaching their sermons	—	—	—	—	√	—	—	—	—	—	—	—	—	—	—
2) Gentiles will come to know God when Jews are redeemed	—	—	—	—	—	—	√	—	—	—	—	—	—	—	—

Medieval Jewish Polemical Literature on Jeremiah 31:31–34

SOURCES (ARRANGED CHRONOLOGICALLY)

1. Saadia ibn Yussif al-Fayyumi (882–942; Egypt, Palestine, Babylonia), *Kitāb al-'Amānāt wa'l-'I'tikādāt (Book of Doctrines and Beliefs),* written in 933; translated by Samuel Rosenblatt (*Saadia Gaon: The Book of Beliefs and Opinions*, New Haven: 1948), p. 167.
2. Jacob b. Reuben (twelfth century; southern France, Spain), *Milḥamot HaShem* (*Wars of the Lord*), written in 1170; ed. Judah Rosenthal (Jerusalem: 1963), pp. 79, 81–82.
3. Meir b. Simeon Ha-Me'ili (early thirteenth c.; Provence), *Milḥemet Miṣwah* (*Holy War*), witten in 1245(?); second part published in M. Y. Blau, *Shitat Haqadmonim* (New York: 1973), p. 330.
4. Moses b. Naḥman [Nahmanides; Bonastruc da Porta] (c. 1195–c. 1270; Spain, Palestine), *Disputation with Fra Paulo Christiani,* July 1263; in J. D. Eisenstein, *'Oṣar Wikuḥim* (New York: 1928), p. 90; translated in O. S. Rankin, *Jewish Religious Polemic* (Edinburgh: 1956), p. 193.
5. Joseph b. Nathan Official (mid-thirteenth c.; Provence), *Sefer Yosef HaMeqaneh* (*The Book of Joseph the Zealot*); ed. Judah Rosenthal (Jerusalem: 1970), p. 70.
6. Anonymous, *Sefer Niṣṣaḥon HaYashan* (*The Older Book of Confutation*), written in the Rhineland, late thirteenth or early fourteenth c.; ed. David Berger (*The Jewish-Christian Debate in the High Middle Ages*, Philadelphia, 1979), Hebrew section, p. 47; English section, pp. 89–90, and note 20, p. 271.
7. Solomon b. Moses de' Rossi (late thirteenth c.; Italy), *'Edut Adonai Ne'emanah* (*The Testimonies of the Lord are Trustworthy*); ed. Judah Rosenthal (in *Meḥqarim uMeqorot,* vol. 1, Jerusalem: 1967), pp. 382–383, 387, 389, 394, 400.
8. Isaac b. Joseph Israeli (early fourteenth c.; Spain), "Reply to Abner of Burgos" (1334); ed. Judah Rosenthal (in *Meḥqarim uMeqorot*, 1), p. 365.
9. Moses HaKohen of Tordesillas (fourteenth c.; Spain), *'Ezer Ha'Emunah* (*Aid to Faith*), written in 1375–79; ed. Yehudah Shamir, *Rabbi Moses Ha-Kohen of Tordesillas and His Book Ezer Ha'emunah: A Chapter in the History of the Judeo-Christian Controversy, II* (Coconut Grove, FL: 1972).
10. Isaac b. Moses Halevi Efodi [Profiat Duran] (late fourteenth–early fifteenth c.; Spain), *Kelimat HaGoyim* (*Disgrace of the Gentiles*), written in 1397; ed. Frank Talmage (Jerusalem: 1981), p. 31.
11. Ḥasdai b. Judah Crescas (c. 1340–c. 1412; Spain), *Bittul 'Iqaré Dat HaNoṣerim* (*Nullification of the Fundamentals of the Christian Faith*), written in 1397–1398 in Catalan; in Eisenstein, p. 296.

12. Joshua b. Joseph Ibn Vives al-Lorki (late fourteenth–early fifteenth c.; Spain), *Nusaḥ Naketab* (letter to Paul de Santa Maria); in Eisenstein, p. 100.

13. Simeon b. Ṣemaḥ Duran [RaSHBaZ] (1361–1444; Spain, Algeria), *Qeshet uMagen* (Bow and Shield), written in 1423; in Eisenstein, pp. 128–129.

14. Yair b. Shabtai da Corregio (sixteenth c.; northern Italy), *Ḥerev Pifiyot* (*Double-Edged Sword*), written in 1560s; ed. Judah Rosenthal (Jerusalem: 1958), pp. 42, 46, 55, 63, 70.

15. Isaac b. Moses Halevi of Troki (1533–1594; Lithuania), *Ḥizzuq Emunah* (*Faith Strengthened*), written in 1593; (Brooklyn: 1932), pp. 27, 111; translated by Moses Mocatta (London: 1851), pp. 14, 125, 155–156.

16. Azriel Petaḥia b. Moses Alatino, dispute on the eternity of the Torah with Don Alfonso Caracciolo (1617; northern Italy); in Eisenstein, p. 198.

Medieval Jewish Polemical Literature: Niṣṣaḥon Vetus (The Older Book of Confutation)

SECTION 71, ON JER. 31:31ff.

"And I will make a new covenant with Israel and with the house of Judah" [Jer. 31:31]. Here the heretics defiantly say that he prophesied concerning Jesus who, from the time of his birth, gave them a new Torah, the abomination of their baptism instead of circumcision, and Sunday instead of Sabbath. The answer is: With these words they contradict their own Torah, for it is written in the book of their error that Jesus himself said, "I have not come to destroy the law of Moses or the words of the prophets, but to fulfill them. Heaven and earth shall pass, but not a thing shall pass from the words of Moses. Whosoever therefore shall destroy one thing of the words of Moses shall be called the least in the kingdom of heaven" [Matt. 5:17–19]. Yet according to their words, he himself caused the Torah of Moses to be truncated by abolishing circumcision, observance of the Sabbath, and many commandments. For they say, "'And I will make a new covenant with them' [Jer. 31:31]; this is the new Torah. 'And not according to the covenant that I made when I took them out of the land of Egypt' [Jer. 31:32]—and not according to the Torah that I already gave them when I took them out of the land of Egypt." In this way they say that Jesus abolished the entire Torah of Moses. We find, however, that David praised the first Torah, as it is written, "Your word is true from the beginning, and every one of your judgments is eternally righteous" [Ps. 119:160]. Moreover, when he said, "But this shall be the covenant that I will make with the house of Israel" [Jer. 31:33], that is where he should have publicly written that new Torah of Jesus. All he does say, however, is "I will put my law in their inward parts" [ibid]; it is therefore clear that this was said about the Torah that he had already given which they had forgotten and that he was promising that he would write it on their hearts so that it would no longer be forgotten. Moreover, why should he mention the house of Israel and Judah more than other nations?"

(trans. David Berger, in his edition, 1979)

APPENDIX B
Medieval and Early Modern Exegetical Literature on Jeremiah 31:31–34

SOURCES (ARRANGED CHRONOLOGICALLY)

A. SUBSTANTIVE COMMENTS

1. Solomon b. Isaac [RASHI] (1040–1105; Rhineland); no comment *ad loc* (!) cites Sifra, BeḤuqotai, II;5 at Lev. 26:9.
2. David b. Joseph Kimḥi [RaDaK; Maistre Petit] (c. 1160–1235; Provence)
3. Moses b. Naḥman [Nahmanides; Bonastruc da Porta] (c. 1195–c. 1270; Spain, Palestine); relevant comments in Torah commentary, *ad* Deut. 30:6, Lev. 26:16.
4. Joseph b. Jose Naḥmias (fl. 1400–1450?; Spain).
5. Don Isaac b. Judah Abravanel (1437–1508; Portugal, Spain, Italy).
6. David b. Aryeh Loeb Altschuler (early eighteenth c.; Galicia) and son, Yeḥiel Hillel b. David (mid-18th c.); *Meṣudat David.*
7. Samuele Davide Luzzatto (1800–1865; Italy).
8. Meir Loeb b. Yeḥiel Michael [MaLBIM] (1809–1879; Volhynia, Poland, Rumania).

B. GRAMMATICAL COMMENTS ONLY

1. Joseph b. Simeon Kara (c. 1070–1130; Rhineland).
2. Isaiah b. Elijah di Trani, the Younger (d.c. 1280; Italy).
3. Joseph b. Abba Mari Caspi (c. 1280–1340; Provence, Spain, Egypt).

Examples of Medieval Jewish Biblical Exegesis

(1) DAVID B. JOSEPH KIMḤI, COMMENTARY TO THE BOOK OF JEREMIAH, 31:31ff.:

31. *See a time is coming ... new covenant*: Its novelty lies in the fact that it will endure and not be broken as was the covenant made by God with the

Israelites at Sinai. And as regards someone (i.e., the Christian) who says that the prophet (here) foretold a new Torah which would be given in the future—not like the new Torah which was given at Sinai, since he (Jeremiah) says, *It will not be like the covenant I made with their fathers*—and that this (new Torah) is the Torah which he (Jesus) gave to them (the Christians), this is the refutation: Behold, he (Jeremiah) himself explains in what way (the new covenant) is *not like the covenant I made with their fathers*—namely, that in that case *they broke my covenant,* but this new covenant will not be broken because *I will put my Torah in their* hearts (*inmost parts*) *and I will inscribe it upon their hearts* so that it will never be forgotten by them. And the entire matter is explained in context—that the novelty of the covenant refers only to its permanence (not its content). And Malachi, the seal of the prophets (i.e., the latest canonical prophet) at the conclusion of his words says, *Be mindful of the Torah of my servant Moses whom I charged at Horeb with laws and rules for all Israel* (3:22)—and this entire passage refers to the messianic future, since he concludes (immediately thereafter), *Lo I will send the prophet Elijah to you (before the coming of the awesome and fearful day of the Lord*; 3:23). So you see that there will never be a new Torah, only that Torah which was given at Sinai, as is written, *whom I charged at Horeb (with laws and rules for all Israel).*

(My translation)

(2) Moses ben Naḥman, Torah Commentary, to Deut. 30,6:

AND THE ETERNAL THY GOD WILL CIRCUMCISE THY HEART. This following subject is very apparent from Scripture: Since the time of Creation, man has had the power to do as he pleased, to be righteous or wicked. This [grant of free will] applies likewise to the entire Torah-period, so that people can gain merit upon choosing the good and punishment for preferring evil. But in the days of the Messiah, the choice of their [genuine] good will be natural; the heart will not desire the improper and it will have no craving whatever for it. This is the "circumcision" mentioned here, for lust and desire are the "foreskin" of the heart, and circumcision of the heart means that it will not covet or desire evil. Man will return at that time to what he was before the sin of Adam, when by his nature he did what should properly be done, and there were no conflicting desires in his will, as I have explained in *Seder Bereshith* (Gen. 2:9). It is this which Scripture states in [the Book of] Jeremiah, *Behold, the days come, saith the Eternal, that I will make a new covenant with the house of Israel, and with the house of Judah; not according to the covenant that I made with their fathers etc. But this is the covenant that I will make with the house of Israel after those days, saith the Eternal, I will put my Law in their inward parts, and in their heart will I write it* (Jer.

31:30–32). This is a reference to the annulment of the evil instinct and to the natural performance by the heart of its proper function. Therefore Jeremiah said further, *and I will be their God, and they shall be My people; and they shall teach no more every man his neighbor, and every man his brother, saying: 'Know the Eternal;' for they shall all know Me, from the least of them unto the greatest of them* (Jer. 31:32–33). Now, it is known that *the imagination of man's heart is evil from his youth* (Gen. 8:21) and it is necessary to instruct them, but at that time it will not be necessary to instruct them [to avoid evil] for their evil instinct will then be completely abolished. And so it is declared by Ezekiel, *A new heart will I also give you, and a new spirit will I put within you; and I will cause you to walk in My statutes* (Ez. 36:26–27). The *new heart* alludes to man's nature, and the [*new*] *spirit* to the desire and will.

(trans. Charles Chavel, 1976)

Example of Early Modern Jewish Biblical Exegesis

MEIR LOEB B. YEḤIEL MICHAEL (MALBIM), COMMENTARY TO THE BOOK OF JEREMIAH, 31:31ff.:

31. *See, a time is coming . . . when I will make a new covenant*: (In the future a new covenant will be necessary) because the previous convenant was made conditional upon their not sinning, which would break the covenant, and because in the past it was possible to sin, but in the (messianic) future it will not be possible to sin at all, as will be explained below.

32. *It will not be like the covenant I made with their fathers*: who at that time were not yet ready for (moral) wholeness and perfection. That was in the time *when I took them by the hand to lead them out of the land of Egypt*—I forcibly took hold of them to remove them (from Egypt) before the appropriate time, since they were not yet (morally, religiously) suited/worthy. But I had to bring them out (at that time) lest they become totally depraved. *A covenant which they broke*: since their natures were still susceptible to evil and they had free choice, and the covenant was conditional (upon their behavior), they broke the covenant when they violated the conditions (in disobeying God's commandments). *And I was lord over them*: forcibly.

33. ***But such is the covenant . . . I will put my Torah in their inmost being***: so that they will observe my Torah out of the urgings of reason until it becomes second nature to them, a part of their very being. ***And I will write it upon their hearts***: There will be no need to write it with ink on paper because it will be written on their hearts—since the heart generates the power to choose and the power of restraint (governance) in the soul—such that the desire to choose the opposite of what the Torah mandates will never arise, because their hearts will be filled with the Torah's statutes, engraved upon their hearts . . .

(My translation)

MICHAEL J. COOK

8. *The Ties that Blind: An Exposition of II Corinthians 3:12–4:6 and Romans 11:7–10*

I admit at the outset of my remarks that I feel odd offering exegesis of texts from a corpus of Scripture not my own. My commitment to New Testament studies, while genuine, is nevertheless that of the historian. In so far as exegesis is commonly construed as partaking of homiletical explication, it is to my own Scripture that I more comfortably gravitate.

I vividly recall the experience of a rabbinic colleague who unexpectedly found himself in what some might construe a similar kind of circumstance. During a televised interfaith panel, he was pointedly asked: "Rabbi, when would you draw an idea for one of your sermons from a specifically New Testament text?" He responded that, in deciding upon a sermon theme, he would, of course, first consult the weekly Torah portion, together with its associated reading from the Prophets; failing that, he would automatically move to the instructive commentators on the Bible, the medieval exegetes Rashi, Ibn Ezra, Naḥmanides, and Sforno, and thereafter to the midrashic commentaries, subsequently (if necessary) consulting pertinent aggadic traditions ensconced within the vast tomes of the Talmud; yet remaining available would be the countless works of later rabbinic literature, plus actual sermons produced closer to the modern day. Culminating his response was a concession: if at *this* juncture he still had discovered no sermonic theme, he might refer to those teachings of Jesus which, if genuine, would no doubt replicate Pharisaic teachings of his day.

At issue here is a problem of asymmetry when it comes to the role and place of Scripture in our respective traditions. We Christians and Jews share in common one corpus of Scripture, but not a second. Our task this afternoon asks of us a direct focusing on that second, and it was to me that the courtesy of choosing the texts for discussion was extended. My own preference was to select passages which in turn draw us to material in our shared Scripture, thus allowing all of us in a sense to focus on both testamental traditions simultaneously. And yet, out of courtesy to Professor Buchanan, I have delineated passages considerably broader in scope than the narrower frame of verses I had in mind, so as to afford him a wider latitude of material should the adjacent verses prove more interesting to him than what my own taste dictated.

•

The specific theme I wish to address is the Pauline allegation of the blindness of the Jews, common to the two passages I have drawn first from II Corinthians and then from Romans. Accusations of "blindness" are a fundamental obstacle to dialogue, for they are predicated not only on the assumption that the other party is impervious to obvious truth, but also on the possibility that such opaqueness is a permanent condition. Given that our common Scripture specifically forbids the setting of an obstacle before the blind,[1] it is sobering to regard an allegation of blindness as itself an obstacle! Must our loyalties to our respective traditions become translated into an imperviousness to the integrity of one another's preachment? Must our bonding and banding together with co-religionists force us to deny that *other traditions* have insight, and require as well that *we* shut *our* eyes to the integrity of others' preachments? Must the "ties that bind" become ties that blind?

The motif of the Jews' blindness is most imaginatively treated by Paul within our selection from II Corinthians 3:12–4:6—

> Since we have such a hope, we are very bold, [13]not like Moses,
> who put a veil over his face so that the Israelites might not see the end
> of the fading splendor. [14]But their minds were hardened; for to this day,
> when they read the old covenant, that same veil remains unlifted, because
> only through Christ is it taken away. [15]Yes, to this day whenever Moses
> is read a veil lies over their minds; [16]but when a man turns to the Lord
> the veil is removed. [17]Now the Lord is the Spirit, and where the Spirit
> of the Lord is, there is freedom. [18]And we all, with unveiled face, beholding the glory of the Lord, are being changed into his likeness from one degree of glory to another; for this comes from the Lord who is the Spirit.

> Therefore, having this ministry by the mercy of God, we do not lose heart. [2]We have renounced disgraceful, underhanded ways; we refuse to practice cunning or to tamper with God's word, but by the open statement of the truth we would commend ourselves to every man's conscience in the sight of God. [3]And even if our gospel is veiled, it is veiled only to those who are perishing. [4]In their case the god of this world has blinded the minds of the unbelievers, to keep them from seeing the light of the gospel of the glory of Christ, who is the likeness of God. [5]For what we preach is not ourselves, but Jesus Christ as Lord, with ourselves as your servants for Jesus' sake. [6]For it is the God who said, "Let light shine out of darkness," who has shone in our hearts to give the light of the knowledge of the glory of God in the face of Christ.

Convinced as Paul is of the New Covenant's vast superiority over the Old, his intimation that Moses himself shared this same awareness is both apt and startling. Jewish Scripture does relate that Moses' face shone when he came down Mt. Sinai and that, in connection with this radiance, Moses put on a veil. Yet precisely *why* he did this remains unspecified in the Exodus tradition.

Paul, however, professes to know the reason: Moses' intent was hardly to shield the Israelites from the glare of the splendor radiant on his face; rather it was to conceal from them the reality that that splendor was already beginning to fade. Indeed, the fading had progressed to the point that Moses' concern, to be exact, was to prevent the Israelites from seeing "the *end* of the fading splendor"!

To be sure, while that initial splendor did indeed signal the Old Covenant's authentic derivation personally from God, Moses himself was already aware that the new legal order he was just now establishing was inadequate and transient, unlike the glory proffered by the newer and permanent dispensation represented by the Christ. "Just as a candle seems to give no light when held in the full light of the sun, so the lesser splendor of the old legal order pales away and seems as nothing in the presence of the new spirit-filled order of the Christian fellowship."[2]

Paul stresses, therefore, that Christian leaders need not fear that what was true in Moses' case will likewise be true in theirs. Since the glory which is seen in Christian teachers is permanent, no one will ever see it vanishing. While Moses "covered with a veil the reflexion of the Divine glory which shone in his face, . . . it is with unveiled face that Christians reflect the glory of Christ and make known their changed condition with openness and boldness,"[3] for like mirrors they reflect on their face the divine glory that Paul has seen "in the face of Christ,"[4] such splendor being not merely a surface reflection or transformation, but rather a transfiguration through and through. Since *their* preachment is splendrous permanently, there is no question of their having to display either the caution or the concealment practiced by Moses.

It is regrettable but true, Paul avers, that that veil, first mentioned as placed over Moses' face, continues, metaphorically speaking, to be worn by later Jews, including those of Paul's day, attesting to their willful ignorance which keeps them from understanding their own Scripture, from properly discerning its actual fulfillment in Christ. Now, "the existing veil does not lie on the head of Moses, hiding the vanishing . . . glory of the Law, but [rather] on the hearts of his people, hiding the dawn of the glory of the Gospels."[5]

Only through belief in Christ, Paul insists, is that veil removable. Noting that, whenever Moses returned to the Lord to speak with him anew, Moses then did indeed take off his veil, Paul implies that only by the Jews' turning in faith to the Lord Jesus Christ will the veil that obscures *their* vision be lifted, enabling them correctly to decipher their Scripture, and clearly to recognize the true relation which the Mosaic order bears toward the New Covenant that supersedes it.

Such, then, is one ready interpretation of what Paul has in mind when he cites this episode. While this interpretation is probably the one to be preferred, note should be taken of an alternative mode of understanding Paul. The previous explanation, the norm, is a kind of typological exegesis which, broadly construed, suggests that "the NT writers found all the main patterns for God's act in Christ already existing in the OT: the clue therefore to the NT writers' interpretation of the OT lay in the recognition of the fact that they were seeking to lay bare in the OT that pattern of divine action which was fully accomplished in the new dispensation."[6] Applied to the episode in question, Paul saw in Moses' fading radiance and the motif of the veil imagery revelatory of the superiority of Jesus and the new dispensation over Moses and what he bequeathed.

Would Paul, however, have been content to rest within the bounds of such interpretation? More far-reaching is the suggestion that Paul must have believed the pre-existent Christ to have been *actually present* within the episodes related by Jewish Scripture. In other words, we are not dealing here with mere symbolism or foreshadowing. The correspondence between experiences of the Christ in the New Testament and events rooted in the Wilderness period lies not in typology, but rather in the reality that the Christ is the prime mover in the happenings of both Testaments!

In I Corinthians 10:4, for example, when alluding to the rock which burst in the Wilderness, Paul does not identify that rock as a type of, or a foreshadowing of, or symbolic of the Christ. Rather he advances the puzzling claim: "and the Rock was Christ"! Some have argued that we have in Paul far more than merely isolated instances of this manner of exegesis. A. T. Hanson maintained that "the normative approach of the NT writers to the OT is not that of typology but rather that of what . . . [may be] called 'real presence'," [7] such that "we shall penetrate nearer to the center of Paul's thought if we drop the conception of types altogether, and think rather of Christ really present at the Red Sea as in the wilderness." [8]

Functioning centrally in such exegesis is the disposition of some scholars to construe appearances of *Kyrios* in the LXX as references to the Christ, reserving *Theos* as allusive to God the Father. Accordingly, Biblical episodes such as our Exodus narrative highlighting *Kyrios* become interpretable as accounts of the activities of the pre-existent Christ. Problematic, however, is our inability confidently to determine how early this type of exegesis was prevalent, or even to ascertain whether early LXX manuscripts did indeed use *Kyrios* in lieu of the Tetragram.[9] To be sure, in later times we encounter this type of exegesis frequently, noteworthy most especially in the *Homily on the Passion,* wherein Melito, addressing Israel, asserts that it was *the Christ* "who led thee down into Egypt and guarded and nourished thee there. He it was who gave thee a guiding light in the pillar and sheltered thee in the cloud, who cut the Red Sea in two and led thee through and destroyed thy enemy. He it was who gave thee manna from heaven, who gave thee drink out of the rock, who gave thee the law on Horeb, who gave thee the land for thine inheritance, who sent forth prophets to thee, who raised up kings for thee. . . ." [10]

Were we to presume that *Paul himself* espoused this mode of exposition in the case under discussion, then the following explanation would suggest itself: In interpreting the glory that shone on Moses' face, Paul understood the conversation which Moses held to have been not with God the Father but rather with the pre-existent Christ instead, there in the Tabernacle in the Wilderness, occasioning also the attendant conclusion that it was the pre-incarnate Christ himself who had appeared to Moses on Mt. Sinai, and the pre-incarnate Christ himself who had delivered to him the Law!

The consequence of such an interpretation would be that what Moses was concealing from the Israelites was not the fading away of the *splendor of the Mosaic legislation* but rather the *evidence that he had encountered and conversed with the Christ,* that evidence being the glory resplendent on Moses' face! It becomes incumbent upon those urging this interpretation also to furnish the rationale for why Moses would have attempted such concealment. The reason forthcoming would have to be that the time for the Christ's self-revelation was only earmarked for much later in history, ultimately as a consequence of the Incarnation of the Word.

As we learn from Romans 11, it was first necessary for God temporarily to allow "a hardening to come upon part of Israel," in accordance with the Divine plan which would permit Gentiles to have opportunity for recognizing the Christ prior to Israel's universal acceptance of him. It was therefore vital that the Israelite people be prevented from discerning *prematurely* the Christ's actual appearance to Moses in the Wilderness, for that would have disrupted the proper sequence of the stages of the Divine plan! Since that time was not yet at hand, what Moses primarily wished to avoid was the children of Israel prematurely recognizing *from the glory on his face* that he had been conversing with the Christ. Hence he shielded his face with a veil! In such an interpretation, if Moses were a prototype, it would not be of the Christ but of Paul, for what Moses had felt constrained to conceal with a veil Paul was himself now revealing!

To render this interpretation more plausible, proponents would have to offer a revised understanding of the word *telos* in II Cor. 3:13. *Telos* would no longer signify the "end" of the fading splendor but would constitute rather a reference to the Christ himself, as we learn from its usage elsewhere (in Romans 10:4) where *telos* is applied by Paul to the Christ as the "end" of the Law.[11] So rendered, therefore, Paul's view would have been that what Moses wished to conceal with his veil was evidene of the presence of the pre-incarnate Christ!

To be sure, there are problems with either of these two major interpretations of what Paul had in mind, the first asserting that Moses used a veil *to conceal the end of the fading splendor of the Mosaic Law;* the second arguing that Moses used a veil *to conceal that he had been conversing with the pre-incarnate Christ.* Not only does the Exodus account not suggest that the splendor on Moses' face was in any way diminishing (*that* is a Pauline innovation), but the Exodus narrative makes it exceedingly clear that the transfiguring of the flesh on Moses' face was actually already fully discerned by the Israelite people *before* the artifice of the veil was introduced. So whatever Paul alleges that veil was intended to conceal had already been observed by the people earlier, *before* the veil could serve its alleged function! Further, the Hebrew suggests that each time Moses spoke with God and thereafter relayed the communication to the Israelites, Moses' veil was *off,* to be restored only *after* Moses was done speaking. For Paul's interpretation of Moses to be compelling, regardless of which of the two understandings of Paul we bring to bear, Moses' veil would have actually had to be in place during Moses' moments of conversing with the Israelites, and this was not the case! It can only be concluded that both understandings of Paul's interpretation are flawed, most likely because Paul's own understanding of the Exodus account is forced.

•

In turning our focus now to the matter of *Jewish* reaction to Paul's exegesis of Scripture, let it first be noted that Paul's interpretation of Moses' radiance emerges as but one of a far wider spectrum encompassing many other explanations informed by Bible study, anthropological and comparative religion findings, and rabbinic thought. To begin with, brilliance of light, a common motif in biblical traditions, often is suggestive of God's presence, most notably in the traditions of the Burning Bush and the pillar of fire. Possibly, it underlies as well the origin of the image of the halo. In the case of Moses' resplendence, the Exodus narrative may imply that the people simply could not manage to gaze at it *steadfastly.* Accordingly, the purpose of Moses' veiling his face would fundamentally have been to spare the Israelites the *strain* of enduring the unveiled rays of divine glory, possibly because the reflection of the divine glory was too *sacred* to be gazed at by human eyes.

The ostensible homiletical lesson of the Mosaic episode is that the greater our union with and our knowledge of God, the more like God we become. The narrative gives us "a beautiful symbolic expression of the truth that close converse with God illumines the soul with Divine radiance, and that those who 'with unveiled face' behold spiritually as in a mirror the glory of the Lord, are gradually through its influence transformed more and more completely into His likeness."[12]

Thus, Moses' face becomes resplendent by virtue of his prolonged and intimate contact with Yahweh. Possibly, the veil motif was derived from the mask of Egyptian (and perhaps also Mesopotamian) priests, whereby they assumed the "face" of the god. Indeed, cultural anthropology and studies in comparative religion do furnish a plethora of suggestive explanations at variance with Paul's narrower albeit imaginative exegesis. The shining of Moses has been posited as an influence of Assyrio-Babylonian religion (particularly its solar elements) which came to conceptualize God as a dazzling radiant being (similar to the gods of the Assyrian pantheon, particularly the sun god Shamash).[13] As for the veil, among primitive priesthoods, veils have served as a kind of mask worn as protection against demons and also to safeguard the common people from the excessive holiness of the priest, not to mention the priest in his approach to the god. Here, of course, it is instructive that Moses confronts Yahweh with his *face uncovered*! While in the ancient Near East a mask was sometimes worn by the priest when communicating the Divine message to the people, here the reverse is true: Moses *removes* the veil when speaking in God's name!

The two most famous artistic renditions of Moses' radiance are, of course, by Rembrandt (Berlin Museum) and Michelangelo (Church of St. Peter in Chains, Rome). While in the former Moses holds tablets of black stone, which are engraved in gold letters, in the latter Moses is sculpted with horns protruding from his forehead.[14] Some exegetes would argue against too readily dismising the idea of Moses' horns as a mere misunderstanding occasioned by the Vulgate's presumably incorrect translation which read "his face had horns."[15] In this connection, Theodore Reik,[16] for example, believed that "horns" reflected an intuitive understanding of the totemistic nature of the Sinai event, related to the Mediterranean myth of the struggle of the hero against the monster, in this case Moses' ascent of Mt. Sinai to fight the totem animal of the Israelites, the bull. Conquering the bull, Moses burned it and thereafter gave its remains to the Israelites, thereby reenacting the totem feast. Moses' victory over the bull, an animal with horns, was signalled by his becoming horned himself!

Extending this listing of alternatives to Paul's exegesis are the admittedly fanciful suggestions from the rabbinic tradition, beginning with one to the effect that Moses' face shone, so the Israelites could deduce from Moses' facial expression the nature of the Torah—the radiance of his face intimated that the Torah which he was imparting was itself likewise full of light![17] Since, we are further instructed, the scroll on which Moses wrote was itself made of fire,[18] when Moses lifted the pen he was using to write, and dried it by passing it through his hair, beams of splendor thus came to attach themselves to his forehead.[19] More charming still is the idea that, when God betrothed Israel, God, as the bridegroom, was responsible for paying the fee to the scribe who drew up the legal documentation. God's payment to Moses, the scribe, took the form of imparting to him a lustrous countenance.[20]

The purpose of listing all these interpretations as alternatives to Paul, some albeit far less compelling that others, is to demonstrate the remoteness, in the Jewish view, of the meanings Paul specifically insists upon. While Paul's right to interpret Jewish Scripture is not to be gainsaid (he himself being Jewish, and the Jewish Bible being his only Scripture), yet reactions critical of his arbitrariness remain in order—especially because his interpretation emerged as symptomatic of the type of exegesis which has redounded severely to the detriment of Jews throughout the ages, spawning as it has ideas which generated antipathy over the entire course of Christian-Jewish relations.

For aside from Paul's arbitrary assertion that Moses wore a veil to obscure from the Israelites either the transient worth of the Sinai revelation or a premature awareness that Moses had encountered the Christ, Paul allows the veil which began on the face of Moses subsequently to waft down and settle as an obscuring blanket on the heart and cognitive powers of the Jewish people themselves, with the inability of the people to see eventually becoming construed as symptomatic of their willful ignorance. Such a notion may very well be responsible for the subsequent depiction—in the history of art—of the Synagogue wearing a blindfold, a stereotype which powerfully determined perceptions by the Christian masses of Jews and Judaism throughout the Middle Ages and even into modern times.

In this respect, our passage from II Corinthians is in consonance with the selection from Romans:

> What then? Israel failed to obtain what it sought. The elect obtained it, but the rest were hardened, as it is written,
> "God gave them a spirit of stupor,
> eyes that should not see and ears
> that should not hear,
> down to this very day."

> And David says,
> "Let their table become a snare and a trap,
> a pitfall and a retribution for them;
> let their eyes be darkened so that they cannot see,
> and bend their backs for ever."

To be sure, this latter paragraph is couched within the wider context of Romans 9–11, in which Paul does manifest, sometimes even poignantly, the depth of his feeling respecting his Jewish roots and fellow people. Yet the essence of his argument in Romans 9–11 sounds to Jewish ears like the following:

The fulfillment which Jews have been seeking throughout their history has actually already taken place, but the Jews have failed to recognize what they have waited so long to see. Blindness in itself is unfortunate, but blindness to the fulfillment of one's own heritage is a tragedy beyond comprehension. The Jews were not chosen because of any merit, for election is not the result of anything we can do to deserve it. It was accorded the Jews only by the free choice of God. Yet what cannot be won by merit can indeed be forfeited by negligence, and not only can election be forfeited, but, in the case of the Jews in particular, it indeed has already been forfeited. The Gentiles, who never pursued righteousness, have attained it, whereas the Jews, who have always pursued it, have missed it altogether. The Jews have been blind all along to the meaning of righteousness—the status which God confers on those who humbly receive it through faith as a gift—and have erroneously assumed that righteousness is a kind of life we can succeed in attaining based on obedience to the Law.

In one respect, it is hardly fair of Jews today to hold Paul responsible for where his views led others. After all, Paul had no awareness that his Epistles would later achieve compilation, not to mention inclusion in a new corpus of what was to be accorded the status of Scripture. Moreover, Paul could not have anticipated that his assertions to the effect of Israel's rejection was only temporary would evolve into a later conviction by others that she had never been the elect,[21] and into the subsequent accusation that God's particular relationship to Israel was in essence to her disadvantage and damnation.[22] Paul could not have realized that the blindness he felt was only temporary in the Jews would be construed by later Christian writers as a permanent affliction. Rather these reinterpretations of Paul were traceable to three root causes of later decades.

One was the unavoidable observation, after Paul's death, that Jewish resistance toward Christianity was showing no signs of abatement; accordingly, it was becoming increasingly difficult to accept Paul's contention, in Romans 9–11, that some day the Jews would after all cease to be blind, and would at last accept Jesus as the Christ. Second, Paul himself had been a Jew, and thus there had been in his case a strong measure of positive personal orientation toward those who were his fellow Jews; but this was a positive kinship with Judaism which later Christian spokesmen did not and could not share. A third and undeniably central factor in these later developments was the calamitous fall of Jerusalem and the destruction of the Temple in the year 70 CE, events heralded throughout the Roman Empire as the triumph of Jupiter over the God of Israel, but serving Christianity in particular as an astounding confirmation of the rejection of the "Old Israel" and the replacement of the Jews by the Christians as the "New Israel." While Paul considered the rejection of the Jews, and more specifically their blindness, to be only temporary, and looked forward to their eventual salvation,[23] the destruction of the Temple was an event so catastrophic in nature as to imply the permanence of the Jews' blindness and of their rejection, not to mention the intensity of divine wrath against God's people.

In spite of these allowances, however, Jews generally must conclude that Paul's orientation, if not anti-Jewish, is at the very least mistaken, and that his sentiments lent themselves to the anti-Jewish applications which were developed by later exegetes of his writings. Most especially did the motif of *blindness* which Paul fosters in both our passages emerge as virulent in later centuries. And while some allusions to blindness even in our two passages at hand may be more preferably rendered as "hardening," whether they be "hardening" or "blindness," both terms express the Jews' insensibility to the truth of the gospel.[24]

To be sure, the image of blindness is hardly unusual, let alone Paul's contribution or innovation. Blindness was, and remains, a very common affliction in the Near East—with bleary-eyes, encrusted with dried secretion and fly-infestation, aggravated by the glare of the sun and irritated by dust-laden winds, constituting a stereotypical condition among all Near Eastern peoples, and hence affording an image for ready appropriation by ancient writers (such that the words "blindness" or "blind" occur eighty-seven times in the Jewish Bible and the Christian Testament). Some have argued that the condition is present even where not explicitly mentioned. Leah's "weak-eyes" (Genesis 29:17), for example, may have resulted from a minor form of trachoma or of ophthalmia which caused redness of the lids and loss of the eyelashes.[25] Even the *metaphoric* application of blindness is surely not Paul's invention. Imputation of blindness was favorite imagery of especially the Hebrew Prophets who applied it as descriptive of the unrighteous and the idolatrous of their day. Indeed, it is to their credit that Hebrew writers incorporated the motif of blindness into the process of the *self*-criticism of their people.[26]

What is unjust is the appropriation of this Jewish imagery against Jews by non-Jewish exegetes after Paul, an application for which Paul himself is at root partly accountable. While later tradition held that Jesus is the true Light which lights every person who comes into the world, such that there inheres in human nature the capacity of spiritual vision, it is unwarranted to allege that this capacity in the Jews, whether by disuse, abuse, or perversity, has become so radically corrupted as to result in Jews' imperviousness to what it is claimed Christians see as intuitively obvious.[27]

> [There followed at this juncture in the presentation the displaying of samples from medieval Christian art wherein the theme of the *blindness of the Jews* was prominent, and no doubt played a critical role in the indoctrination of the illiterate masses, for whom such artistic representation may have functioned as the primary pedagogical tool of the Church. Representative samples may be found in W. Seiferth, *Synagoge und Kirche im Mittelalter* (Munich: Kösel-Verlag, 1964).]

In summation, therefore, the reality has to be grappled with that, what Paul construes to be blindness, Jews consider to be their *clear-sightedness.* It is interesting that, as the Torah draws to a close, it sees fit to remind us not only that "never again did there arise in Israel a prophet like Moses—whom the Lord singled out face to face," but that, unlike the cases of Isaac, of Eli, of David, of Ahijah, the eyesight of Moses never dimmed in spite of his old age: "Moses was a hundred and twenty years old when he died; *his eyes were undimmed*" (Deuteronomy 34:7). In this connection, it is fitting to cite the debate our Rabbis tell us once transpired between Moses and Adam:

> Adam said to Moses: "I am greater than you because I have been created in the image of God." . . . Moses replied to him: "I am far superior to you, for the honor which was given to you has been taken away from

> you, as it is said [in Psalm 49:13], 'But *Adam* abideth not in honor'; but as for me *the radiant countenance* which God gave me still remains [unabated!] with me." . . . For it is said [in Deuteronomy 34:7], 'His eye was not dim, nor has his natural force abated'."[28]

As if in answer to Paul, rabbinic Judaism insisted that Moses' countenance was not fading and has not faded; in no sense had he been engaged in *veil*ing from his people any *fading* of his dispensation.

Indeed, our rabbis instruct us, it had only been when God had placed Moses in the cleft of the rock and had covered him with the Divine hand until God had passed by,—only then had it been, as a consequence of having been covered by God's hand, that Moses' face had first become resplendent,[29] implying in effect that only after God has passed us by can we discern evidence of God's having been present with us.

In pursuance of this metaphor, Judaism holds that often we can glimpse truth not at the moment itself but mainly, as it were, in retrospect—that perhaps we can detect the traces of God's presence not at the moment itself, but only when we look back on history. In so doing, we who seek to discern truth from the vantage points of our respective traditions, may we seek to combine with one another in our separately achieved perceptions of when God has been most manifest in past history, merging the results of our discoveries, pooling rather than polarizing our representations of truth. And in so doing may we take comfort and find meaning in the ties that ***bind***, but always be wary of the ties that ***blind***!

Notes

1. Leviticus 19:14.

2. F. V. Filson, "II Corinthians: Exegesis," *Interpreter's Bible*, Vol. X (Nashville: Abindgon, 1953), p. 309

3. A. Plummer, *A Critical and Exegetical Commentary on the Second Epistle of St. Paul to the Corinthians* (*International Critical Commentary*; New York: Charles Scribner's Sons, 1915), pp. 105ff

4. II Corinthians 4:6

5. Plummer, op. cit., p. 101

6. A. T. Hanson, *Jesus Christ in the Old Testament* (London: S. P. C. K., 1965), p. 4

7. Ibid., p. 8

8. Ibid., p. 13

9. See G. Howard, "The Tetragram and the New Testament," *Journal of Biblical Literature* 96 (1977), pp. 63–83; idem, "Phil 2:6–11 and the Human Christ," *Catholic Biblical Quarterly* 40 (1978), pp. 381ff; also F. Hahn, *The Titles of Jesus in Christology: Their History in Early Christianity* (New York: World, 1969). I acknowledge appreciation to David Williams for directing my attention to the bibliography on this problem.

10. Section 84. Ed. Campbell Bonner as No. XII in *Studies and Documents,* ed. K. Lake and S. Lake (London & Philadelphia: 1940); translation by A. T. Hanson.

11. References to "fading" in II Corinthians 3:7,11,13 (varying forms of *katargeisthai*) would thus preferably be construed as "to be annulled" or "rendered ineffective"; cf. Hanson, op cit., p. 27

12. S. R. Driver, *The Book of Exodus in the Revised Version*, with introduction and notes (Cambridge, 1911), ad. loc.

13. J. Morgenstern, "Moses with the Shining Face," *Hebrew Union College Annual* 2 (1925), pp. 8–9

14. The Vulgate renders *cornuata facies* as requiring understanding of horns; even the Rabbis may have been aware of the problem, identifying (albeit playfully) "the horn of Moses" as one of ten horns in the bible (*Lamentations Rabbah* II, 6).

15. The root *qrn* means "to shine" (cf. especially Habakkuk 3:4: "And a brightness appeareth as the light; *rays* hath He at His side" [JPS, 1955]).

16. *Ritual: Psycho-Analytic Studies,* trans. D. Bryan (London: Hogarth Press, 1931), pp. 354ff

17. *Exodus Rabbah* XXXIII, 1

18. *Deuteronomy Rabbah* III, 12

19. *Exodus Rabbah* XLVII, 6

20. *Deuteronomy Rabbah* III, 12

21. *Epistle of Barnabas,* 14

22. Justin Martyr, *Dialogue with Trypho,* 16, 18.

23. ". . . all Israel will be saved; as it is written. . .," Romans 11:26 (RSV).

24. Cf. W. Sanday and A. C. Headlam, *A Critical and Exegetical Commentary on The Epistle to the Romans* (*International Critical Commentary;* New York: Charles Scribner's Sons, 1895), pp. 313ff; also C. A. Beckwith, "Blindness," *Dictionary of the Apostolic Church,* J. Hastings, ed., Vol. I (New York: Charles Scribner's Sons, 1916), p. 153

25. A. Macalister, "Medicine," *Dictionary of the Bible,* J. Hastings, ed., Vol. III (New York: Charles Scribner's Sons, 1900), p. 331

26. See the excellent discussion of self-criticism in Jewish Scripture presented in the recent volume by Norman A. Beck, *Mature Christianity: The Recognition and Repudiation of the Anti-Jewish Polemic of the New Testament* (Selinsgrove: Susquehanna University Press, 1985), pp. 11ff

27. Cf. A. Miller, "Blindness," *Dictionary of Christ and the Gospels,* J. Hastings, ed., Vol. I (New York: Charles Scribner's Sons, 1911), p. 214

28. *Deuteronomy Rabbah* XI, 3

29. *Exodus Rabbah* XLVII, 6

GEORGE WESLEY BUCHANAN

9. Paul and the Jews (II Corinthians 3:4–4:6 and Romans 11:7–10)

Introduction

There is a common thread running through the two texts considered here. That is God's rejection of all but a remnant of the Jews. An examination of these passages will involve Paul's use of scripture and his understanding of Jewish law and tradition. Although Christian and Jewish history shows that we have devoted an excessive amount of time and energy to insulting and fighting each other, there were many basic points on which early Jews, Samaritans, and Christians agreed. This made argument possible.

PAUL'S METHOD

Paul did not construct his arguments out of thin air. He took the terms of his polemic right out of the texts of Jeremiah and Exodus, and interpreted them to his advantage, just as other lawyers did in his day, and as lawyers still do today. Both Paul and the rabbis were legalists, apologists, or jurists. They were not objective analysts. They did not begin by looking for an unknown solution. Each began with a case to defend, a conviction to persuade, an argument to win. They studied the law and earlier precedents to prove that something they wanted to defend was legally true, even though it may actually have been false. This required them to accept certain rules of rhetoric that were dogmatically determined, such as: 1) Everything that is in the world is in the Scripture;

therefore the *Tanak* is the only valid source of information. 2) All prophecy is prophesied only for the days of the Messiah (*San* 99a); since Jesus was the Messiah, any prophecy found in the *Tanak* could be applied to Jesus. 3) Time moved in repeatable cycles, so that which was happening could be paralleled by some earlier event, and, on the basis of the earlier event, discovered in greater detail.[1]

Since two witnesses were required in court to prove a case, Paul started his argument with both Exodus and Jeremiah as his proof. This not only included two texts, but one of these was from the Torah and the other from the prophets. When Paul presented his case, he followed normal rules of rhetoric, using data taken right out of the approved code of law, or taking terms that reasonably belonged in the context.

For example: Paul got the expression, "new contract" from Jeremiah 31:31. Jeremiah, in turn got his authority from Exodus 34. Paul used texts from both sources. From Exodus 34, Paul took the expressions "tablets," "glory," "the face of Moses," "the glory of his face," "Moses placed a veil upon his face," "the sons of Israel," "receiving mercy," "contract," "turning to the Lord," "the veil taken away," and "shining." Other idioms, like "to this very day" and the use of the terms "life" and "death" metaphorically, are frequently found in Deuteronomy, and the word, "walking" used to mean manner of behaving, and the idiom, "hardening of hearts" or "minds"[2] are expressions that frequently occur in the *Tanak*. In twenty short verses, Paul utilized all of these biblical terms in a typically midrashic manner.

Literary Forms

Scholars like Windisch[3] have identified Second Corinthians 3:7–18 as a Christian Midrash. That there is midrash here is without question, but it is not so clear that Windisch has accurately circumscribed the unit. The theme "boldness" seems to be emphasized there, but it is also found in 3:4 and continues up to 4:6. Second Corinthians 4:7 seems to be a continuation of 3:3, which applies these arguments for support and guidance in daily living.

Within the unit, 3:4–4:6, there seems to be another self-contained passage, outlined as an inclusion by the words, "Lord" and "Spirit":

> The Lord is the Spirit,
> where the spirit of the Lord is is liberty,

and all we with unveiled face,
seeing the glory of the Lord as in a mirror
are being transformed into the same image
from glory to glory,
just as from the Lord, the Spirit (3:17–18).

This is a rather poetical unit which Paul may have taken from early Christian liturgy, or he may have composed it himself. In either case, it is coherent with the rest of this message.

The argument given here is very similar to that which Paul gave to his other major letters, and the terminology is the same. For example, the word "spirit," which occurs frequently here, is found a total of ninety times in Romans, Galatians, and the Corinthian correspondence, and the word "glory" occurs thirty-eight times in the same documents. Paul also frequently presented his case in court terms, such as righteousness and unrighteousness or vindication and condemnation, that occur in this unit. The vocabulary and argument in this passage are so clearly Paul's that it is fair to deduce part of the meaning here from Paul's message in general, i.e., the *perat* from the *kellal.*

Paul's Situation

Second Corinthians 3:4–4:6 seems to have been an argument Paul had developed and used before. Because he needed to illustrate the greater importance of human beings to letters of recommendation, Paul evidently pulled this argument on the relationship of the letter and the spirit out of his file and used it again here (cf. Rom 7:6).

This argument reflects Paul's position against the judaizing Christians in general. Paul had been on the defensive, evidently because judaizing Christians had entered his territory, and tried to persuade the members that Paul was not a valid apostle for these reasons: 1) An apostle was an agent who was legally identical to the principal who sent him. The English word, apostle, comes from the Greek *apostolos,* which represents the Hebrew *šaliaḥ*, "a sent one," meaning a legal agent who has been sent to perform a mission on behalf of the principal. As the rabbis said, a man's agent is like the man himself. Anyone claiming to be an agent had to have the acknowledgment of the principal that he was an accredited apostle. Since Paul never met Jesus in the flesh, it was held that he was not a valid apostle.[4] 2) Paul did not require circumcision as the *Tanak* commanded, and, 3) judging from Paul's response, some people had said Paul's gospel was "veiled."

Paul had just succeeded in regaining the support of the Corinthians after a long, intense conflict and period of estrangement. Once the Corinthian Christians were again on Paul's side, Paul set out to provide them with defensible, legitimate arguments to support and sustain this position, which had finally become both his and theirs. In so doing, he contrasted their position with that of the Judaizers on several points that he considered important.

Special Terms

There are several special terms which Paul repeated throughout this pericope. Some of these are: 1) boldness, 2) contracts, 3) ministry, 4) glory, 5) liberty, 6) face, and 7) the god of this age. These are interwoven throughout the Corinthian passage in a literarily effective, midrashic manner, contrasting some Christians to some Jews, typologically, from a certain Christian point of view. These terms will be examined in order:

Boldness

The Israelites were afraid and ashamed after the incident of the Golden Calf. Moses had to veil his face before the Israelites could look upon that which was destined to be annulled, because their minds were hardened (3:13–14). In Exodus 34, it was Moses' *face* which was too bright for the Israelites to gaze upon, but Paul seems to have transferred their inability to look at the human being, Moses, to being unable to look on the contract Moses gave. This legal switch implies that the Pentateuch was called "Moses," even in that early date. Already in the *Tanak,* the Pentateuch was called "the book of Moses" (Neh. 13:1; 2 Chron. 25:4). Paul claimed that until his day, the same covering remains upon the reading of the old contract (3:14).[5]

There may have been a liturgical practice in Paul's day that prompted this accusation. For example, those who read from the Scripture may have covered their face with a veil before reading it, out of respect and deference. This would have been similar to the practice of the High Priest, when he entered the Holy of Holies. He first burned incense to create a cloud, so that he would not see the Lord face to face (*Yoma* 5:1). The prayer shawl may have been a thin veil through which a person could read. Before reading, the shawl might have been placed upon the head with part of it covering the eyes.[6] This, of course, is only an imaginary guess, which may never have actually been practiced. Whether there was any kind of liturgical practice or not, Paul's meaning is clear. He meant by this that Jews still did not know how to read and understand the old contract. This old text was not uncovered or unrolled for the Jews, because Christ had annulled it (3:14).

Whereas Jews were kept away from the glory by a veil, members of the new contract were not veiled, according to Paul. Christians do not have to be timid, afraid, and ashamed, since they have such a glorious hope. In fact, Paul said, "We have renounced the hidden things of shame" (4:2). He also said, "We experience great boldness," (3:12) and "we all with unveiled face, seeing the glory of the Lord as in a mirror, are being changed into the same image from glory to glory, even as from the Lord, the Spirit" (3:18). By describing Christians as those who see the glory of the Lord with an "unveiled face," Paul meant that Christians have the status of Moses before the Lord. Although Israelites could not even look at Moses with unveiled faces, Moses could approach the altar, and see the glory of the Lord without a veil. Likewise, Christians have the veil removed. Since they benefited from the Messiah's merit, their sin and shame from the Golden Calf has been removed. Whenever parties to the old contract turned to the Lord, as Moses had done, they, too, could see the glory of the Lord without a veil. At this stage, however, their "turning to the Lord" involved their becoming Christians, according to Paul. It also involved their turning away from the other Israelites, as Moses had done, but Paul did not mention that.

Scholars have argued whether the word "Lord" here means "God" or "Christ." Since the Messiah was the legal agent of the Lord, the result was the same. The word "Lord" was used because the text in Exodus 34 had said "Lord." The term "lord" was a normal title of address for a king or messiah. Medieval Jews called their messiah, David Alroy, "Our Lord, our king, the Messiah of the Lord."[7]

Rabbis used an idiom that was similar to the one Paul expressed to interpret the Israelites leaving Egypt "with a high hand" (*beyad râmâh*), which, they said, means "with an uncovered head" (*ber'ōš galûy*) (Exod. 14:8 Mek *beshalaḥ* 2.231–32). With these associations, the expression "with unveiled face" seems to mean "with pride, arrogance, confidence, or boldness," and supports Paul's earlier statements: "Such confidence as this we have" (3:4), "We experience great boldness" (3:12), and the later statement, "We do not lose heart, but we have renounced the hidden things of shame" (4:1–2).

What could Christians see with unveiled face that Jews could not? Paul probably took this to mean the basic point of his gospel: God's righteousness was obtained through faith, according to the promise given to Abraham (Gen. 15), rather than by the zeal of Phinehas (Num. 25). Paul probably meant that Jews still understood the meaning of the scripture the way Paul himself understood it when he was still a zealous Pharisee. In those days he had persecuted the church of God and plundered it. He advanced in Judaism above his contemporaries, so exceedingly zealous had he been for the traditions of his fathers (Gal. 1:13–14).

At that time, Paul's theology and ethics followed the type of Phinehas, who was so zealous for his tradition that he killed Zimri and his new Midianite wife, to prevent law-breaking and mingling with the Gentiles. This was reckoned to Phinehas as righteousness (Num. 25:1–13; Ps. 106:30–31). The only other place in the entire *Tanak* where anything was reckoned as righteousness was Abraham for his faith (Gen. 15). Paul's conversion meant he stopped preaching righteousness by zeal, and began preaching righteousness by faith. Had God's word given only one example of that activity which passed the divine court, the goal might have been clear, but there were two. Paul subscribed first to one and then to the other. Historically, both had been successful.

Observing righteousness of zeal, Israelites acquired the Promised Land, under the leadership of Joshua, David, and Solomon. Mattathias led the Hasmonean rebellion, "being zealous for the law just as Phinehas had done to Zimri" and calling all those who were zealous for the law to follow him (1 Macc. 2:26–28). Abraham did not act in the same way. He simply believed that God would fulfill his promises, and this was reckoned righteousness. In Babylon, Jews suffered for their sins without zeal and retaliation, and, according to the promise given to Abraham, this was reckoned to them as righteousness, and the land was restored without Jewish bloodshed.[8]

To understand the importance of Paul's message of salvation by faith, it is necessary to realize that he was preaching against the doctrine of salvation by zeal. Once he had been enlightened by the doctrine of salvation by faith of Abraham, and accepted the Messiah as the suffering servant whose merits would cancel Israel's sins, he thought his former fellow believers in salvation by zeal were still in the dark, reading the text with their eyes blinded. Whereas Paul was telling people to leave vengeance to the Lord, and render no one evil for evil, the majority of Judaism was plotting ways to overthrow the Romans by military force. Paul assumed, of course, that, if Jews would turn the other cheek, walk the second mile, and provide hospitality needs for enemies, God would do the dirty work and heap coals of fire upon the Romans' heads (Rom. 12:14–21).

Urbach listed a number of arguments various rabbis used in their contest between the view that Jews must first repent and then the Messiah would come, and the opinion that the Messiah would come and redeem Israel without repentance. These are basically continuations of the conflict between Phinehas and Abraham theology, or the conflict between zeal and faith as that which is necessary for righteousness. Urbach correctly judged that Paul came out on the side of those who thought the Messiah would come and turn away the transgression of Jacob (Isa. 59:20; Rom. 11:26). In fact Paul thought the Messiah had already come while Jews were still in their sins, and he voluntarily died in their behalf to turn away their sins.[9]

When Paul told of his deep longing and prayers offered to God in behalf of the Jews for their salvation, he said, "For I testify with respect to them that they have the zeal of God, but not according to knowledge, for they do not know the righteousness of God, but they are trying to establish their own righteousness (Rom. 10:2–3). Following the doctrine of the righteousness of Phinehas, they were misdirected. They were reading Moses with a covering over the text. Paul and other Christians, however, knew the correct reading of the law. They, with unveiled face, beheld the glory of the Lord.

There is nothing more humane about the passive doctrine of conquest than the military doctrine of conquest. The goal was the same. The only reason Jews would be willing to accept suffering without retaliation was their belief that if they piled up enough credits in the treasury of merits this way, God would afflict the Romans in a more vicious way than the Jews were capable of doing. There was textual and historical justification for the doctrine of righteousness of faith, but this was a minority point of view. It did not have enough influence to prevent the all-out war with Rome in 66–72 or 132–135 CE any more than the 5% of Japanese who were pacifists before World War II had been able to prevent that war. Paul correctly said that Jews were looking for a sign, something like the plagues of Egypt or the miracles of the wilderness, and the Greeks wanted wisdom. Christians preached that Christ was crucified according to a suffering servant theology and the faith of Abraham. This was to zealous Jews a stumbling block and to Greeks, nonsense, but to those who believed in the righteousness of faith, namely the elect or called ones, both Jews and Greek, a crucified messiah was both the power and wisdom of God (I Cor. 1:22–24). The merits of his undeserved punishment were enough to turn away the sins of Jacob (Isa. 59:20).

There were some, obviously the zealous followers of Phinehas, who thought Paul and the passive Christians were traitors, just as Jews earlier thought Jeremiah had been, and, after the last Passover with Jesus, Peter and Judas probably concurred with others that Jesus was a traitor, saboteur, or fifth columnist.

These zealous nationalists thought Paul should be ashamed, timid, and reticent for his doctrine of passivity in a national crisis, but Paul responded that he was not ashamed of the Gospel. It was the power of God for salvation to all who believed as Abraham had done, for the righteousness of God was revealed from faith to faith (Rom. 1:16–17), i.e., from the faith of Abraham to the faith in Christ. It was in defense against zealous attackers that Paul claimed Christians are justified in being bold before God; they could approach Him with unveiled face, because they did not have a covering over the text. They had the true faith, the right doctrine. After the fall of Jerusalem and the defeat of Bar Cochba, many more Jews and Christians believed Paul's argument than during his lifetime.

The New Contract

The contract which God made with the Israelites had already been annulled once in the wilderness. When the people worshipped the Golden Calf, Moses broke the tablets, marking an end to the contract. After the people had become ashamed of their action, Moses pleaded with the Lord not to destroy this people. Moses' conversations with the Lord sometimes took place on the mountain and sometimes in the tent of meeting (Exod. 33:7–11). Moses asked to see God's glory, but the Lord refused. Instead of God's face, Moses was permitted only to see His back (Exod. 33:17–23). God then agreed to make a new contract with Moses and the people (Exod. 34:10). The terms were specified: 1) For the Lord's part, He would perform miracles for the Israelites and drive out the inhabitants of the land for them. 2) The Israelites agreed to observe the sabbaths and set feasts, and keep the commandments Moses had copied on the tablets (Exod. 34:10–28).

The contract the Lord made with Israel was accepted by Jeremiah (31:32), Ezekiel (16:8), and Second Isaiah (54:5) as a marriage contract, with the Lord as the husband or *baal,* and the Israelites as the bride (Isa. 54:5, Jer. 31:32; Ezek. 16:8). Deuteronomy had given the conditions by which a husband could divorce his wife and annul this contract. He had to put the charge into writing, place it in the wife's hand, and send her out of his house (Deut. 24:1).

On the basis of Deuteronomy and Leviticus, Jeremiah concluded that Judah had broken the contract, just as Israel had done. Israel had been sent away (Jer. 3:8), a sign that she had been divorced, and Jeremiah said Judah had sinned worse than Israel. Therefore, God would also divorce Judah and send her out of his house. This would annul the contract made at Sinai. Once the Jews had paid off their obligation at half-wages, however, Jeremiah, like Hosea, was confident that God would again woo His people in the wilderness and make with them a new contract, so that they would be His bride, and He would be their husband (Hos. 2:14–23; Jer. 31:31).

The new contract that Jeremiah promised was one claimed by sects of Judaism of later times. One sect that resided in Damascus considered itself the people of the new contract, excluding all the rest of the Jews and Israelites (CDC. 7:19; 3:12–20). Members of another people of the new contract were later also called Christians.

The author of Hebrews referred to the term "contract" seventeen times, and spoke of Jesus as the mediator of a new contract (Heb. 9:15), noting that since God had said through the Scripture that this was a new contract, He meant that the other contract was old (Heb. 12:24). Paul used the expression nine times, and even without using the term, referred to the contracts under which Jews and Christians lived as marriage contracts (Rom. 7:1–6), and their attachment to the contracts, as either freedom or slavery (Rom. 6:15–23).

When Paul wrote II Cor. 3–4, he followed Jeremiah in referring to the contract at Sinai as one written on tablets of stone (Jer. 31:33; II Cor. 3:3), an old contract (3:14) that was being annulled (3:14),[10] and a contract that kills (3:6). The new contract, on the other hand, was not written in ink, but on the tablets of the human heart; it was not of the letter which killed, but of the spirit which gave life.

The word "spirit" is not the opposite of law. It would take a more extensive study than this to discover its full range of meaning, but the word "spirit" seems to have had some legal force that could be related to a legal contract. For example, when the spirit fell upon various charismatic leaders prior to Saul, they received authority to become tribal leaders (Jdgs. 6:34; 11:29; 13:25; 14:6, 14:19; 15:14). The spirit of the Lord came upon Saul (1 Sam. 10:6; 11:6) and David (1 Sam. 16:13), and they became kings; it also departed from Saul, as Saul began to lose his authority (1 Sam. 16:14). When Moses appointed judges, and gave them authority to perform their offices, the Lord took some of the spirit that was upon Moses and gave it to the judges (Num. 11:16–17). The literature that was legally the word of God was called inspired or "inspirited."

When Jesus gave the twelve the authority to become his apostles, he comanded them to receive the Holy Spirit (John 20:21–22). Paul said the various offices of the Christian leaders had been given with the same spirit (I. Cor. 12:3–13). Paul told the Corinthians that he was present with them in spirit when he authorized them, while his spirit was there, to expel a member from their congregation (I Cor. 5:3–5). When Christian leaders laid their hands upon people, they received the Holy Spirit and became Christians at the same time (Acts 8:15–17). The word "spirit" seemed to be related to legal authority. It was also related to life. Just as breath was necessary for physical life, so spirit was necessary for legal or religious life, and the word "life" was important to Paul's argument. The spirit was sometimes also identical with the Lord. In the little poetic pericope, the first line said, "The Lord is the spirit," and the inclusion was closed with phrase, "just as from the Lord, the spirit" (3:17–18).

None of the prophets concluded that the divorce between the Lord and His people was the last word. Jeremiah said God would establish a new contract and renew His relationship with His people. Second Isaiah said there never had been a legitimate divorce. God had sent His people away, to be sure, but He had not given them a legal document to say they were divorced. Therefore, they could assume that they were still within the legal terms of the original contract (Isa. 50:1).

When calling the old contract one of judgment or condemnation, Paul meant that it had been tried in the divine court and legally invalidated. Paul followed Jeremiah in claiming that the old contract had been abolished, and a new one had been made. Like Jeremiah and the author of Hebrews, Paul argued that the new contract was a superior document. Like Jeremiah, Paul held that it would be permanent. Also, like Jeremiah, he believed that it would include all Israel. Jeremiah said it would include not only Jews, but also Samaritans, and Paul argued strongly that, when the Jews turned to the Lord, their veil would also be removed (II Cor. 3:15–18), and both they and the Gentiles would be included.

Paul also faced the possibility that God might again annul the contract with His people, as He had done at least twice before. Alongside the word "boldness," which Paul used, was the word "hope" that the new contract would be permanent (II Cor. 3:12). If the members of the new contract were not faithful, then they also would be sent away from the Lord's house (Rom. 9–11). On the basis of a whole florilegium, Paul argued that Israel was guilty, but Paul was as unwilling as Jeremiah to admit that Jews had stumbled so as to fall permanently (Rom. 10:5–11:12). Israel could always count on the redeeming remnant. This was the opinion of Amos (9:8–9), Micah (2:12; 5:3), Zephaniah (3:12–13), Jeremiah (23:3) and Ezekiel 14:14–20). There were among the Jews an antitype of the seven thousand Elijah saw who had not bowed the knee to Baal (Rom. 11:1–10). These were the true elect who would turn to the Lord and become Christians. In turning to the Lord, they were doing just as Moses had done (Exod. 34:34). When Moses turned away from the Israelites, he turned to the Lord. Paul did not say that turning away from the Israelites was a necessary part of turning to the Lord, but the text could have been interpreted that way to explain what happened to the Jews when Christians turned to the Lord. Such rejection, however, was self-imposed. Jews might also turn to the Lord as Moses had done, and be included among the elect. In fact, Paul thought all of this was part of God's design, which also included the readmission of the Jews (11:11–32). Since Paul did not say this, we are dealing in speculation, but to follow the typology of Moses fully would include noticing that, when Moses turned away from the Israelites, he did not turn away permanently. He continued in communication, without ever abandoning these people. Whether or not Paul justified his logic from this text, the conclusion he reached is the same. Paul was just as confident as the

Rabbis that all Israelites have a portion in the age to come (San. 10:1; Rom. 11:26).

The use of "life" and "death" in the Scripture had a more significant meaning than that which can be determined by pulse and breath. It referred to membership in the contract community. Moses warned the Israelites to keep the commandments of the contract so that they might live (Deut. 4:1). Those who held fast to the Lord were alive (Deut. 4:3). Those with circumcised hearts were alive (Deut. 30:6). God set before the Israelites life and good, and death and evil (Deut. 30:15). Those who were faithful to the contract had the good life, whereas the others were dead. Bishop Serapion identified the living with the elect.[11] When Jesus said that the dead should bury their own dead (Matt. 8:22; Lk. 9:60), he did not mean corpses should bury corpses. These were religious terms, distinguishing members from non-members of the contract community. Just as breath gave people life, so the spirit provided life for the community of the contract.

Paul argued that since the old contract had been annulled, it therefore "killed" those bound by it, and provided them a ministry of death (3:7). The new contract, on the other hand, was not written in ink, but on the tablets of the human heart; it was not of the letter which killed, but of the spirit which gave life (3:6). This was the only valid contract, and its members were the only ones who had life.[12] This judgment was taken from the Prophet Jeremiah, and was therefore "proved" by early Jewish and Christian standards.

Glory

Paul might have argued further that Moses was not able to see the Lord's glory, whereas those of the new contract were, but he chose instead to contrast the glory of the old with the new in *qal waḥômer* arguments: If the ministry of death, which was being annulled and was carved as letters in stone, came in such glory that the Israelites could not bear to look into the face of Moses, then how much more would the ministry of the spirit, which was alive, continuing, and in effect abound in glory (3:7–8).

Moses was only allowed to see the glory of the Lord as the Lord was leaving. This justified Paul in calling this annulled or cancelled glory (3:8, 13) and constrasting it with permanent glory instituted by the new contract. Evidently answering an accusation that the gospel was also veiled,[13]

Paul conceded that it was, but only from the members of the old contract, to keep them from seeing the light of the gospel of the glory of Christ (4:3–4). The God who made light shine in darkness has shined in the hearts of the members of the new contract, to give light of the glory of God in the face of Christ (4:6). Paul here compared the light of the days of creation with the light of the days of the Messiah.

The RSV's translation of Second Corinthians 3:18 as from "one degree of glory to another" misses the point of the contrast. Others have offered such solutions as from the glory of Moses to the glory of the Spirit, from the glory lost in Paradise to the glory received in heaven, glory of this world to glory of the next, glory of the temporarl to the glory of the eternal.[14] The more likely solution is that the contrasting glories are those of the old contract mediated by Moses to the new contract mediated by the Messiah, since these are the basic typological contrasts of Paul's argument.

Transferring from the glory of the old contract to the glory of the new implies that members of the Corinthian community had originally not been uncontaminated Gentiles, but were instead members of the old contract. When they became Christians, they were changed from the members of one contract to the members of the other and at the same time were also changed from the annulled glory to the permanent glory, according to Paul.

There are other reasons for thinking that Pauline Christians had mostly come from diaspora Judaism. Rabbis said the term "uncircumcised" was used to mean people outside the Promised Land, circumcised or not, and "circumcised" described people inside the Promised Land, circumcised or not (Ned. 3:11). When Paul, Peter, James, and John divided up the civilized world for their ministry, it was agreed that Paul would go to the uncircumcised, and Peter, James, and John would go to the circumcised (Gal. 2:7–9). This seemed to have been a geographical division, placing the entire diaspora under Paul's authority.[15]

Although Paul was called the apostle of the Gentiles, it is clear that there were circumcised Jews among his congregations (I Cor. 7:18–19); Gal. 5:6; 6:15; Col. 3:11). Before the ministry of Paul, the physically uncircumcised members of the communities were also probably people who had been trained in Jewish communities and accepted into the membership, without the requirement of circumcision. Otherwise it would have been humanly impossible for Paul to have converted a territory almost identical with modern Turkey in eleven short years. This would only have been possible if Paul went only to communities that were already trained in Jewish traditions and scripture, so that he had only to convince them that Jesus was the Messiah they had already been trained to expect.

These were the ones who gave up their ministry to the old contract to become ministers of the new contract (3:15–18). All of this came from the Lord, according to Paul—not from the apostles of circumcision. All of this glory that was evident to the members of the new contract had already been annulled with the old contract that was out of date.

Ministry

Those who thought Paul was an invalid apostle, who could not have been acknowledged by Jesus, whom he had never seen in the flesh, claimed that he had no legal credentials. These were told that Paul and his fellow Christians had been qualified by God Himself, as ministers of the new contract in the spirit which gives life, in contrast to the old written code which kills (3:6).

In his use of the term "ministry," Paul held that those bound by the new contract were ministers of this contract, and their life was a ministry. This was not a ministry of death, carved on tablets of stone, but a ministry of the spirit which was associated with glory. This ministry, when tested in the divine court, was judged innocent and just, in contrast to the ministry of the old contract which was condemned by the same court (3:9). Therefore it far outshines the old ministry in glory (3:10). Corinthian Christians, therefore, have this ministry, just as they have received mercy from God. Because of this, they should not lose heart but rather have confidence.

Freedom

Paul said there was freedom wherever the Spirit of the Lord could be found (II Cor. 3:17). He also indicated that Christians had this freedom, when he said that they saw the glory of the Lord with unveiled faces (3:18). The freedom of which Paul spoke was not civil liberty. This was the liberty that came with Sabbath or Jubilee release, when debtor captives had their debts forgiven and were allowed to return to their own land and people. Under the Pentateuchal laws governing debtor justice, this would only be possible on certain conditions: 1) if the debtors had worked off their indebtedness at half-wages, thereby paying double for all their sins; 2) if the Sabbath or Jubilee arrived, so that their debt could be legally cancelled; 3) if someone acted as a redeemer and bought the slave from the creditor, and released him or her; 4) if the creditor forgave the debt and released the slave.[16]

When Jesus, as the Messiah, had accepted undeserved crucifixion and death, Paul believed that he had acted as the redeemer, paying off all of Israel's debt of sin (Rom. 5:6–11), just as twentieth-century Jews believe that the Jews who died in the Holocaust acted as redeemers for modern Jews, thus being responsible for the establishment of Israel as a state. Because Jesus had redeemed Christians, Paul told the Corinthians that they had been bought with a price. Therefore they were not their own. The freedom that came from their being bought did not mean they were released from the authority of the purchaser (I Cor. 6:19–20). Being free means being a slave of Christ (I Cor. 7:23–24). Jesus was also interpreted as the sin offering necessary for atonement on the Date of Atonement (Lev. 4:27–35; Yoma 8;8). Rabbis decreed that the sin offering effects atonement on the Day of Atonement, and can effectively cancel sins that the Jew has committed against God. On that day, the sin offering would also cancel the sins of a believer against his fellow Jew, but only if the believer had become reconciled to his fellow believer by obtaining forgiveness from all his sins (Yoma 8:8–9).

Paul believed that Jesus was the sin offering required for atonement; he was the redeemer that had paid for Israel's sins, and by so doing had reconciled the accounts between God and His people (Rom. 3:24; 5:6–11, 16–17). Those who were members of the new contract could benefit from this redemption and obtain this freedom (Rom. 3:26; 4:24–25; 6:7, 18–23; 8:2, 21; I Cor. 1:30; 6:19–20; 7:22–23; Gal. 4:5). All that was left to complete these benefits of atonement was for Jews to become reconciled to one another. Paul was engaged in the ministry of reconciliation in an effort to make this possible. He told the Corinthians, "All this is from God who has reconciled us to himself through Christ and has given us the ministry of reconciliation" (II Cor. 5:18; also 5:19).

Face

Consistent with his policy of contrasting the situation related to Moses and the Israelites at Sinai with that related to Christ and the members of the new contract, Paul observed that the Israelites were the

Christians who saw the glory of the Lord with unveiled faces. Although the members of the old contract could not gaze upon Moses' face, God shone in the hearts of the members of the new contract, so as to illumine the glory of the knowledge of God in the face of Christ. This provided the parties to the new contract with a superior position in relationship to Christ than the Israelites had had with Moses. The point of Paul's discussion was to contrast Christ to Moses, and the Israelites to Christians in relation to the term "face."

The God of this Age

Basic to early Judaism and Christianity was a doctrine of two ages: in one of these, the Gentiles ruled, and in the other, Jews ruled.[17] The age between the fall of Jerusalem in 586 BCE and the rededication of the Temple in 164 BCE was the captivity, the Greek age, the evil age, the age of slavery, the beasts, and the Gentiles. The god of that age was an enemy of the Jewish god and was incarnate in Antiochus Epiphanes. The Hasmonean age was the age to come; it was ruled by Jews, and the god of that age was the Jewish God, incarnate in the various Hasmonean leaders. In Paul's time, Rome ruled Palestine, and Paul called that period "this age" (I Cor. 1:20; 2:6). It was also thought of as the evil age and the captivity. Another early Jew called Beliar the "ruler of this world" (Asc. of Isa. 4:2). Jews considered themselves in slavery, regardless of their financial situations, as long as some other power ruled the Promised Land. The god of this age, then, was the god of the Romans, and it was incarnate in Caesar. There was probably no doubt at all in the minds of Jews and Christians about what Paul meant when he used this expression.

Jews and Gentiles

Paul's Judgement

It is not difficult to understand what Paul meant in Rom. 11:7–10. He clearly distinguished the elect, who were Christians, from the rest who were hardened. The elect were those who had turned to the Lord and accepted the new contract. The Jews, who had not accepted the new contract, were the ones who were hardened. This means God had hardened their hearts just as He hardened the heart of Pharaoh. Like a good lawyer, Paul brought to the argument three legal witnesses to prove his case: Deut. 29:3, Isa. 29:10, and Ps. 69:22–23:

Near the end of his life, Moses spoke to all the Israelites, reminding them of the miracles and providential care the Lord had provided for them. Yet he lamented: *The Lord God has not given us a heart to know, eyes to see and ears to hear, until this day* (Deut. 29:4). In a prophecy of doom against Jerusalem, Isaiah warned that the Lord would send armies of the enemies to surround Jerusalem, but the Israelites would not be able to defend themselves against these enemies, because *The Lord has poured out upon you a spirit of deep sleep. He has closed your eyes* (the prophets) *and covered your heads* (the seers) (Isa. 29:10). The third text came from a Psalmist who claimed that he had been falsely accused (Ps. 69:4). He asked not only that the Lord vindicate him, but that the Lord punish his accusers severely:

> *Let their table become a snare before them!*
> *Let their sacrificial feasts become a trap*
> *Let their eyes be blinded so they cannot see.*
> *make their loins tremble constantly* (Ps. 69:22–23).

Paul took these three texts, all of which had originally been directed against some, at least, of the Israelites. Furthermore, they represented all divisions of the *Tanak:* The Torah, the Prophets, and the Writings. Therefore they provided legitimate proof that God intended to harden the Israelites' hearts and blind their eyes. Paul spliced these sentences together to say the following:

God had given them (Deut. 29:3) *A spirit of deep sleep* (Isa. 29:10), *eyes for* not *seeing and ears for* not *hearing, until this very day* (Deut. 29:3), and David says:

> *Let their table become a snare* and *a trap,*
> a stumbling block and an obstacle
> *Let their eyes be blinded so they cannot see;*
> *Make their loins tremble constantly*
> (Ps. 69:22–23; Rom. 11:8–10).

Like most of his Jewish contemporaries, Paul believed that God had ordained things the way they were. Pharaoh's heart was hard because God hardened it. Like the servant in Isaiah, Paul also believed that God had called him from his mother's womb to preach the good news among the Gentiles (Gal. 1:15–16). Jeremiah promised that the Jews from the North country woudl return (Jer. 31:8). Isaiah promised that someone would publish the good news of salvation (Isa. 52:7). Paul thought he was fulfilling these scriptures in his work in the diaspora. He was trying to get all of the Jews in the diaspora to become reconciled to one another, so that they could benefit from the merits of Jesus' death. Paul earnestly wanted all Jews to respond quickly, become reconciled to one another, so that on the Day of Atonement, the kingdom would come. In actual fact, however, many Jews did not respond. How could that be explained? Since these were the days of the Messiah, and since all prophecy was prophesied only for the days of the Messiah, he had only to look in the *Tanak* to find the answer. Here he had found three texts, one from each division of the *Tanak,* and since it took only two witnesses to prove a case, he should have been able to rest his case with this evidence.

THE JEWS

Why did not all Jews respond? Paul did not list the analytical possibilities. For an apologist, the answer must always presume that the opponents are mistaken. Therefore the apologist looks only for some way to explain the opposition's faulty judgment. Paul found the answer he needed in the Scripture. Jews did not respond, because God had hardened their hearts and blinded their eyes, just as He had done with Pharaoh, and also as He had done at least these three times in the past to which he referred.

Paul did not conclude from this that God had completely rejected His people, any more than Jeremiah or Hosea had. The purpose of this was to enable the Gentiles to be included in the number of the elect. This may be taken to mean that God had given up His tribalistic chauvinism to include the entire world into His family of the elect. Paul may actually have meant that, but he probably did not start his mission that way.

ROMAN CHRISTIANS

However arrogant and offensive Paul's judgments seem to twentieth-century Jews and Christians, apparently it did not seem out of order to Jewish Christians of Paul's day. His letter to Romans was a letter of introduction to a church he had not established. This church has traditionally claimed that Peter was there. This may mean only that it was founded by a Petrine sect of Christianity, and therefore its founding was credited to Peter, just as there are many Lutheran churches in the world where Luther has never been. This church later excommunicated the anti-Jewish Marcion, who had no problem in the Pauline churches of Asia Minor. Paul devoted a large portion of his letter to the Romans, explaining his attitude toward the Jews as if that were necessary. It is therefore reasonable to assume that this was a Jewish Christian church that differed from Paul in some ways. Nevertheless they preserved this letter.

Once any group of people thinks that it alone is the true elect of God, it is not difficult to justify relegating others to a position of exclusion. The good figs are segregated from the bad figs, so too there is the elect within the elect within the elect. That which Paul did was no more chauvinistic than the teachings and actions of Ezra, Nehemiah, Jeremiah, or Second Isaiah. The arrogance that goes with the doctrine of election has splintered Judaism and Christianity into hundreds of divisions, as this *apartheid* doctrine is propagated from generation to generation. From this perspective, Paul's attitude toward other Jews is just about what historians might have expected *a priori* of any Jewish sectarian leader who deviated from his sectarian roots in any important way.

Conclusions

Although the argument which Jews and Jewish Christians used in refuting Paul is not given, it would not be hard to conjecture it. Paul's opponents[18] were just as confirmed followers of Phinehas theology as Paul was of Abraham theology. Since Paul's time both the followers of Phinehas and the advocates of Abraham have continued to survive, both in Christianity and in Judaism, and both might chalk up victories on the basis of historical events. Along with Phinehas theology has come a long history of Jewish and Christian terrorism, and along with the passivism of Abraham theology there continues Jewish and Christian sado-masochism. Both of these exist to this day, and it would be impossible to prove that one was more enlightened than the other, although both groups would be willing to try.

An objective analyst, however, with the benefit of two thousand years of history to examine, might judge that neither group sees the glory of God with an unveiled face, because there is not much that is humane or civilized about the conquest theology on which both groups base their hermeneutics. Those Christians and Jews who hope to remove the veil and gain more insight into the glory of God will have to reexamine some of our basic premises, such as conquest theology and the doctrine of election, with their logical consequences of manifest destiny, racism, chauvinism, and religious *apartheid.* According to Paul, "There is no distinction [whether Jew or Christian] for all have sinned and fall short of the glory of God" (Rom. 3:22–23). Jews and Christians are obligated to begin a new reformation, if we do not wish to be ashamed of our ethics in the twentieth century. We should begin this jointly, from within, and at once.

Notes

1. On this see George W. Buchanan, *Jesus: the King and his Kingdom* (Macon: Mercer U. Press, 1984), pp. 253–283

2. A. Plummer, *A Critical and Exegetical Commentary on the Second Epistle of St. Paul to the Corinthians* (Edinburgh, c1951), p. 98

3. H. Windisch, *Der zweite Korintherbrief* (Goettingen, 1924), p. 112

4. This text alone shows that Paul understood the legal significance of apostleship: He said that he had confidence *through* Christ toward God, meaning that Christ also was an agent or apostle of God, and that God administered His legal affairs through the agency of Christ. Paul also referred to Jesus as the image of God (4:4), probably meaning that he was God's legal agent, His human ambassador, or incarnate apostle. This was the normal status of ancient Near Eastern kings. Paul admitted that he, himself, had no sufficiency of his own, but that his sufficiency or authority came from God who had made him a minister of the new contract (2 Cor. 3:4–6). As an apostle, his authority was delegated to him from that principle.

5. Evidently the earliest extant use of the term "old contract" is this. The word for "old" here is *palaiâs* which does not mean something ancient and revered, but something old and worn out. Heb. 8:13 has the same connotation: "While saying 'new' he makes the first old" (*pepalaiôken*). The sixteenth-century term "convenant" is avoided here, because twentieth-century people are more familiar with the term "contract," which has the same meaning. The Hebrew *berith* can be rendered "contract" and "treaty" everywhere in the Scripture and make good sense.

6. This is a suggestion of Plummer, *ICC II Corinthians,* p. 99. The veil was "not rolled up" (*mê anakaluptomenon*) (3:14). This is a different term from the one used to describe the Christian who saw the glory with "unveiled" (*anakekalummenoi*) face (3:18)

7. George W. Buchanan, *Revelation and Redemption* (Dillsboro, N. Carolina, c1978, now Mercer U. Press), p. 195

8. There was probably very little Babylonian or Persian bloodshed, either. By diverting the river, Persians entered Babylon by surprise, and took the city without a battle (Herodotus, *History* 1.191; Xenophon, *Cyropaedia* 7.V.1–36; A. Leo Oppenheim [tr.] "Babylon and Assyrian Historical Texts," J. B. Pritchard [ed.], Ancient Near Eastern Texts [Princeton: 1969], p. 315. They undoubtedly received a lot of Jewish cooperation in terms of espionage and other intelligence work before and during the event, because Second Isaiah knew Cyrus had plans like these before they had taken place, and he also knew that when Cyrus took Babylon, Jews would be allowed to return to Palestine.

9. E. E. Urbach, "Redemption and Repentance in Talmudic Judaism," R. J. Z. Werblowsky and C. J. Bleeker (eds.), *Types of Redemption* (Leiden, c1970):191–92

10. *katargoumenon* means being annulled, invalidated, or cancelled and not "fading" as RSV, TEV, and NIV render it. Furnish correctly observed that the term was used twenty-seven times in undisputed letters of Paul, always with reference to something that is invalidated or replaced in some way. (V. P. Furnish, *II Corinthians* [Garden City: 1984], p. 203) Lias said that the term meant *to make thoroughly useless or unprofitable,* and hence *to do away with, abolish, bring to naught.* (J. J. Lias, *The Second Epistle to the Corinthians* [Cambridge: 1897], p. 50)

Like Paul, the author of the Hebrews also contrasted the old contract with the new, the old glory with the new, and encouraged confidence and hope (Heb. 3:1–12; 8:6–13). Since the author of Hebrews said that the old contract was growing old and ready to vanish (8:13), scholars have, consciously or unconsciously, attributed the "fading" judgment of the author of Hebrews also to Paul, but Paul did not say the old contract was fading; he said it was being invalidated, just as Jeremiah had done.

11. Deiss, *Springtime of the Liturgy,* tr. M. J. O'Connell (Collegeville, MN: c1979), p. 191

12.See further George W. Buchanan, *The Consequences of the Covenant* (Leiden: 1970), pp. 112–21

13. This may have meant that Paul's gospel was not written. It was a secret or "veiled" gospel known only to the members. There is not much evidence in Paul's letters that this was the case, but there were secret catechisms and gospels among early Jews and Christians in antiquity, so this is a possibility.

14. So Plummer, *ICC Corinthians,* p. 107

15. See further George W. Buchanan, "The Samaritan Origins of the Gospel of John," J. Neusner (ed.), *Religions in Antiquity* (Leiden: 1968): pp. 149–175

16. See George W. Buchanan, *The Consequences of the Covenant* (Leiden: 1970), pp. 9–18

17. George W. Buchanan, *Jesus: The King and his Kingdom* (Macon: 1984), pp. 258–264

18. George W. Buchanan, *The Consequences of the Covenant,* pp. 36–37.

Part IV

Who Speaks for Whom When Judaism and Christianity Meet?

JAKOB J. PETUCHOWSKI

10. *Who Speaks for Whom When Judaism and Christianity Meet?*

There was a joke which made the rounds at the time of the Second Vatican Council. It dealt with a trade-off which the Jews proposed to the Pope. If the Pope were to clear the Jews of the charge of deicide, the Jews, in turn, would give up the first *yequm purqan.* The "first *yequm purqan*" is a prayer in which Orthodox Jews to this day pray for the heads of the academies and for the exilarchs of Babylonian Jewry—institutions which ceased to function about one thousand years ago. (Reform Judaism abolished that prayer in the nineteenth century, and Conservative Jews have changed its wording in such a way that the prayer refers to the scholars of other times and places as well.)

Fortunately, the Jews—at any rate, the Jews living today—were cleared of the charge of deicide. The Church has even emended its Good Friday prayer for "the perfidious Jews." But the "first *yequm purqan*" is still piously intoned, Sabbath after Sabbath, in Orthodox synagogues throughout the world.

The joke which made the rounds at the time of the Second Vatican Council operated on several different levels. There is something funny, at least from the vantage-point of non-Orthodox Jews, in that anachronistic prayer per se, a prayer which invokes God's blessings upon institutions which ceased to exist a millennium ago—and which does so in Aramaic, a language which most Jews understand even less than they do Hebrew. There is something funny in the suggestion that the Church would have had anything to gain by having the Jews give up praying for the religious and secular officials of ancient Babylonian Jewry, seeing that there might well be one or two other components of the traditional Jewish liturgy, which originated in days when Christians were perceived by Jews as enemies and persecutors, and the retention of which today might indeed offend Christian sensitivities, while the removal of those prayers might make some Christians happy.

But perhaps the funniest part of all of this joke was the suggestion that "*the* Jews" could deal with the Vatican at all, as though "*the* Jews" had elected representatives, empowered by all those who call themselves "Jews" to negotiate with the head of the Roman Catholic Church. *That,* more than anything else, made the story into a *joke*—at least in the view of those Jews who understand that Moses was perhaps the last Hebrew who succeeded in charting a common course for all the other Hebrews, or, more accurately, for the majority of them.

After the days of Moses, Israel began a period of life when according to the Scriptures, "they all did what was good in their own eyes."[1] The institution of the monarchy, which was meant to bring some order into the national life, soon enough turned into *two* monarchies: one of Judah and one of Israel. And when the monarchy came to an end, when the Kingdom of Israel disappeared, and the Kingdom of Judah went into Babylonian Exile, we find the exiled Judaeans laying the groundwork of a Religion of the Book, which, after the Return from Exile and the establishment of the Second Commonwealth, would lead to the formation of various different sects, all based on the variety of different ways in which one and the same Book could be read and interpreted. Thus we get the Pharisees and the Sadducees, the Essenes and the Apocalypticists, the Qumranites and the Ebionites, to mention but a few of them. Later generations created the literature of Rabbinic Judaism—Talmud and Midrash, Commentaries and Codes—a literature the most striking feature of which is the constant divergence of opinions leading to an ongoing dialectic, which could only ocasionally be brought to a temporary halt by the recognition of the fact that the views of *both* contending sides represent "the words of the Living God."[2]

When, therefore, the modern Jewish scene affords us the colorful spectacle of Orthodox Jews and Reform Jews, Conservative Jews and Reconstructionist Jews, Synagogue Jews and Non-Affiliated Jews, Hasidic Jews and Secularist Jews, Zionist Jews and Non-Zionist Jews, Socialist Jews and politically Neo-Conservative Jews, and when each of the groups just mentioned has its own subdivisions, then the phenomenon itself is not without historical precedent. Perhaps the only difference between the present situation and the Jewries of earlier generations is that earlier generations were perhaps more likely to establish *some* consensus in religious matters than modern Jews are.

In the past, philosophers and theologians might have argued about the nature of God, about anthropomorphism, and about individual providence. But they *all* believed in God. In the past, the *contents* of revelation may have been the subject of discussion. Was the Written Torah self-sufficient, or did it require for its elucidation an Oral Torah? But the "fact" of Revelation itself was taken for granted. On basics, there *was* a Jewish consensus—as there was on the outer limits beyond which one found oneself ouside of Judaism. That is why, when, in the medieval forced disputations, the Church compelled rabbis to debate Judaism and Christianity with Christian champions, quite frequently Jewish converts to Christianity, the Church could take it for granted that, on this issue, the rabbis chosen would be representative of the Jewish community as a whole. Today *no* rabbi is representative of the whole Jewish community. Indeed, it might even be hard to find a rabbi who is truly representative of his or her own Jewish "denominational" constituency.

The same applies when we go beyond the realm of the synagogue, and look at religiously neutral or secular Jewish organizations. There is *no* Jewish organization, national or international, which represents all Jews, or even only the majority of the Jews, although there are several Jewish organizations which presume to speak in the name of Jewry as a whole. And much as the State of Israel would like to create the impression that *it* represents all the Jews of the world, the fact remains that most of the world's Jews, having been offered the opportunity to become Israeli citizens, have declined that offer, and have proved by their remaining where they are that the government of the State of Israel is not *their* government—however enthusiastically many of those Jews may profess their love for the Holy Land.

This is neither the time nor the place in which to discuss whether this lack of consensus, this absence of an overarching roof organization for all Jews is a good thing or a bad thing. If we were to formulate this as a question, such as: "Would it be a good thing for all Jews to be organized?," we would, when it comes to the answer, merely establish one more division of opinion among the Jews. But good, bad, or indifferent, the fact itself must be noted and understood—if only to facilitate a greater clarity in the Christian-Jewish Dialogue.

Many Jews are at long last beginning to realize that not all Christians are the same, that there are different denominations within Christianity itself, and different trends and tendencies within each of the Christian denominations. Christians, too, must now realize that there is no such body as "*the* Jews," that the Jews among themselves are *at least* as much divided as Christians are among themselves. That is why, before a productive dialogue can take place, *both* sides should establish who is talking to whom. There are, for example, Jewish secularists who, for one reason or another, may seek to engage in dialogue with Christians—just as there are secularists of Christian parentage who, for whatever reason, may be interested in a dialogue with Jews. They should all be encouraged to do so. But, at the same time, when secularists of Jewish parentage have a dialogue with secularists of Christian parentage, what is taking place should not be misconstrued as a dialogue *between Judaism and Christianity.* There are also secularists in clerical garb, real or metaphorical.

Christians should also bear in mind that religious Jews do not necessarily take the same position on all matters under discussion, just as religious Christians are known to differ on matters of both principle and practice. An Orthodox Jew and a Reform Jew may differ as widely as do a liberal Methodist and a fundamentalist Southern Baptist. And I do not wish to complicate matters still further by dwelling on various *political* programs which tend to masquerade as religious issues, and which often tend to obscure the real purposes of Christian-Jewish encounters.

Enough has, I believe, been said to underline the important difference between the kind of religious consensus which made it possible for both Synagogue and Church in the Middle Ages to have their representatives engage in debate, and the kind of almost limitless pluralism which makes it impossible for any one Jewish individual or any one Jewish organization to represent all of the Jews—or for any one Christian individual or any one Christian organization to represent all of the Christians.

Perhaps it may be the very activity of dialoguing with Christians which will one day compel Jews to strive for some kind of Jewish consensus—just as Karl Barth recognized two decades ago that the problem of the Church's relation to the Jews is the most important item on the inner-Christian ecumenical agenda.[3]

In the meantime we have to recognize that those Jews who, in an encounter with Christians, speak for Jews and Judaism, are merely *individuals* who are not necessarily representative of anything or anybody else. Thus, for example, if someone on the lecture circuit in Europe or the United States claims that he, as an Orthodox Jew, believes in the historicity of the physical resurrection of Jesus, no inference may be drawn by his audience either about the nature of the man's professed orthodoxy or about the attitude taken by official Orthodox Judaism towards the Christian claim that Jesus was resurrected from the dead. And if an Israeli journalist, who has done much to facilitate the modern Christian-Jewish Dialogue, informs us that Jesus was "one of the central figures of Jewish religious consciousness," then that journalist is certainly giving testimony to the importance of Jesus to his own Jewish religious life. But he is so far from representing Judaism as a whole that, in this matter, he cannot even be regarded as representative of the particular "denominational" wing of Judaism to which he himself belongs.

One of the pioneers of the modern Christian-Jewish Dialogue was the late Hans Joachim Schoeps (1909-1980). With important studies about early Judaeo-Christianity and about the Apostle Paul to his credit, and with a popular work on the history of the Christian-Jewish Dialogue available in an English translation, Schoeps deserves to be better known than he is by the latter-day practitioners of the dialogic art. It was Hans Joachim Schoeps who said more than a generation ago:

> The twentieth century has seen the disintegration of the traditional spheres of life and doctrine from which, formerly, authorized representatives spoke. Ultimately, authorization to speak is relegated completely to the subjectivity of the speaker. Today no conclusions can be drawn concerning the Christian or Jewish quality of the life of a representative of the Christian or Jewish community on the basis of his office. Therefore, there can be no other authorization, no other warrant, than that which emerges from the life of the speaker and bespoken by the doctrinal content of his life. A Jew and a Christian conduct a Judaeo-Christian dialogue only when the contrasting beliefs of the centuries are brought to bear in their conversation. . . .[4]

Schoeps's reference to the "contrasting beliefs," important as it is to his notion of the authenticity of the respective positions, must not be misunderstood. The one thing that Schoeps did *not* want was the replay of medieval disputations. That is why he also said:

> Whereas in the medieval disputations the delegates of Judaism and Christianity delivered monologues in a "discussion," the outcome of which was already determined before it had begun, in the real dialogue

> of the modern era, something basically new has occurred—the "opponent" has become a "partner," the "monologue," a "dialogue"; creedal dogmas are not expounded, but must be vindicated through the life of the speaker.[5]

What Schoeps seems to be saying, if we understand him correctly, is that the Jewish partner in the Christian-Jewish Dialogue must demonstrate in his or her own life that he or she really believes in Judaism. It is, in other words, no longer good enough solemnly to intone: "Judaism says," or "Jews believe." There must also be some evidence that what "Judaism says" or what "Jews believe" is an actual part of the person's life. Theoretically, but *only* theoretically, this opens up the strange possibility of putting the Christian partner in a position of having to evaluate the Jewish partner's Jewish authenticity. But that possibility would be as preposterous as would be the granting to the Jewish partner of the prerogative to determine who, among Catholics, Lutherans, Anglicans, Methodists and Presbyterians, manifests the highest degree of Christian authenticity.

Nor would the problem be solved by having the presumably "most traditionalist" wing of each denomination determine who or what is a "good Jew" or a "good Christian." For, however valuable a given tradition might be in enlightening us about an earlier stage of religious development, that particular earlier stage is not necessarily typical of the given faith-community as a whole. If, for example, it were to be determined that it is the very nature of Judaism to develop organically from one stage of development to another, then the attempt to "freeze" that process in one of its earlier stages would in itself represent a misreading of the process as a whole. But, of course, the question as to whether or not the Jewish tradition is one of continuous change, is itself a bone of contention within the Jewish camp. And even those who agree that "change" is the name of the Jewish game, do *not* agree on the extent and on the speed of that change, or on what are the permanent elements of belief and practice, as opposed to those elements which are, and always have been subject to change. To base the Jewish contribution to the Christian-Jewish Dialogue on the lowest common denominator among those who call themselves Jews would be to invoke a caricature of Judaism instead of a recognizable Jewish position. There is, after all, a great deal more Jewish authenticity in a multiplicity of strongly held and sharply conflicting

Jewish views than there would be in a compromise statement so watered down that *all* Jews—believers and unbelievers, Zionists and non-Zionists, Orthodox and Reformers—could subscribe to it.

Is it, then, the case that we must accept as "Jewish" or as a "Jewish position" any statement or utterance made by someone known as a Jew? If a Jew tells us that today's weather is nice, does this become a *Jewish* assertion? Or if someone known as a Jew solves the crossword puzzle in today's newspaper, is he or she providing a *Jewish* solution?

Admittedly, we have chosen some far-fetched illustrations. We have done so on purpose, in an attempt to establish the *principle* of the thing. But the principle is the same whether we talk about the weather and about solutions to crossword puzzles, or whether we talk about secularist positions adopted by people known as Jews on such issues as abortion-on-demand and non-denominational prayer in the public schools. That is, if those positions are dictated by commitments to secularism and political liberalism, rather than by the thrust of the millennial Jewish tradition.

We are now ready to revert to two matters which, in different contexts, have been mentioned by us before. One is the pre-condition laid down by Hans Joachim Schoeps for the Christian-Jewish Dialogue today, to wit: that "the contrasting beliefs of the centuries are brought to bear" on the conversation. The other was contained in our very brief survey of the rise of Jewish pluralism. There we had spoken about "the exiled Judaeans laying the groundwork of a Religion of the Book" which led to "the formation of various different sects, all based on the variety of different ways in which one and the same Book could be read and interpreted."

Both of those statements underline the fact that Judaism did not originate today or yesterday. There is, after all, something which, through the centuries and the millennia, has been recognized as "Judaism." And that something, however different its appearance might have been at different times and in different environments, was, at all times and in all places, based on interpretations of the Book, differing, indeed often conflicting interpretations, but always interpretations of the *same* Book. And the Book, however and whenever it came to be written, was perceived as enshrining the constitution of the faith-community of Israel. The range of possible interpretations of that "constitution" was tremendous, even as the "constitution" itself was not all of one piece. After all, the author of the Book of Job argued with the theology of the Book of Deuteronomy—even as, in later centuries, a Rabbi Akiba would derive a different message from the Scriptures than a Rabbi Ishmael did, an 'Anan ben David, founder of the Karaite sect, would understand it diferently from a Sa'adya Gaon, doughty defender of Rabbinism, and, in the nineteenth century, an Abraham Geiger, theologian of the rising Reform movement, would obviously find imperatives in it which a Samson Raphael Hirsch, founder of Jewish Neo-Orthodoxy, was unable to perceive.

What they all had in common, those just named and the numberless exegetes whom we have not named, was the sense of belonging to the Sinaitic Covenant, the willingness to deal creatively with the biblical patrimony, and the endeavor to justify their own positions by an appeal to the Book and its various and diverse interpreters. That sense of belonging, that willingness, and that endeavor, characteristic of the Jewish wrestling with the Book, enable us to speak about a *Jewish* religious tradition in the first place, and, I would submit, provide us with a yardstick we can use to determine the "Jewishness" of any purported Jewish position advanced within the setting of the Christian-Jewish Dialogue.

Briefly put: Whatever is said by a Jew who has a sense of belonging to the Sinaitic Covenant, a willingness to deal creatively with the biblical patrimony, and who endeavors to justify his or her position by an appeal to the Book and its various and diverse interpreters, represents *a* legitimate and authentic Jewish position, which must be appreciated as such by fellow-Jews and by Christian dialogue partners alike.

At the same time, there is no justification whatsoever to generalize from the legitimate "Jewish" position of the *individual* Jew about a position supposedly held by *the* Jews as a whole. Moreover, and this has a bearing on the Christian-Jewish Dialogue, chances are that different Jews will appeal to different stages in the development of the Book and of the literature of its interpreters. This is an inner-Jewish reality, and one which necessarily tends to get reflected in the Christian-Jewish Dialogue.

Judaism has encountered Christianity at various stages of its own and of Christianity's development. For some Jews, the mind-set developed by Jews in response to the Christianity of the second century may be deemed to be adequate to the encounter with Christianity in the twentieth century. Other Jews might prefer to see matters in historical perspective, and to re-examine some issues in the light of present-day realities, both Jewish and Christian. A Jewish judgment on second-century Christianity or thirteenth-century Christianity may or may not be appropriate to twentieth-century Christianity. Jews are liable to differ among themselves on whether earlier judgments are appropriate or not. Much will also depend upon the kind of Christianity with which they are confronted in the "here and now."

A naive formulation of the Christian Trinitarian God concept, for example, which gives the appearance of tritheism, may elicit one kind of Jewish response. A sophisticated philosophical and theological construction of the Trinitarian belief, which is careful not to infringe upon biblical monotheism, may well elicit quite another. The Apostle Paul's Pharisaic contemporaries may have had good reasons to feel threatened by Paul's antinomianism. What is questionable is whether the same reasons hold good when latter-day Reform Judaism encounters Paulinian doctrine. After all, Reform Judaism has its own rather pronounced antinomian tendencies, and it had to bear the brunt of attacks by the defenders of the old-time religion no less severe than those directed against the old Apostle to the Gentiles. Some questions, in other words, may have to be reopened.[6] Some old answers may have been adequate in their own time, but prove to be no answers at all under changed circumstances. At the same time, some *new* answers may be so faddish and so completely bereft of any basis in the millennial Jewish tradition that they can be recognized as little more than the idiosyncrasies of stray Jewish individuals.

And yet, there is a need for *all* answers to be heard and to be evaluated—if only those answers be offered in good faith by those who, in word and in deed, give evidence that they speak out of a commitment to the historic tradition of Judaism, however they construe its mandates for the present, and if only the answers be based on knowledge, and not on ignorance. True as it is that no single Jew has been authorized to speak for Judaism as a whole, it is no less true that, in their aggregate, *all* Jews, whose words are born of commitment, and whose utterances are informed by knowledge of the sources, *all* Jews, in their aggregate, speak for Judaism, however contradictory their interpretations of Judaism may turn out to be.

No doubt, Christian dialogue partners would have an easier time of it, if there were such a person as a Jewish Pope, or if the various organizations, religious and secular, which claim to represent multitudes of Jews, really did represent those multitudes. But, for better or worse, there is no Jewish Pope, and, as the intense rivalry among Jewish organizations—both religious and secular—demonstrates, no single organization has as yet been given a mandate by the majority of the Jews. A colorful pluralism is and remains a fact of Jewish life; and Christians who want to enter into a dialogue with Jews will be able to do so only if they are prepared to face that fact.

Thus the answer, from the Jewish side, to the question: "Who speaks for whom when Judaism and Christianity meet?," is: "No *single* Jew does. But *all* of them do."

Notes

1. Judges 21:25

2. B. *'Erubhin* 13b

3. Cf. Hans Hermann Henrix, "Ökumenische Theologie und Judentum," in *Freiburger Rundbrief,* XXVIII (1976), p. 27

4. Hans Joachim Schoeps, *The Jewish-Christian Argument.* Tr. David E. Green. (Holt, Rinehart & Winston: New York, 1963), p. 127. The first edition of the German original appeared in 1937.

5. Schoeps, op. cit., p. 126

6. Cf. Jakob J. Petuchowski, "Erlösung - Sünde - Vergebung," in Hans Hermann Henrix and Werner Licharz, ed., *Welches Judentum steht welchem Christentum gegenüber?* (Haag und Herchen Verlag, Frankfurt a. M: 1985), pp. 9–18. See also Jakob J. Petuchowski, "Der jüdische Konvertit zum Christentum in jüdischer Sicht," in *Una Sancta,* 40 (1985), pp. 158–168

EMERSON S. COLAW

11. *Why Dialogue?*

We start with a question: Why make the effort to engage in dialogue? One suggestion is that dialogue is the clarification and fulfillment of God's will of which holy purpose Judaism and Christianity are surely related parts.

Second, "Because of their common roots and intertwined histories, Christianity cannot fully understand itself without Judaism, nor can Judaism fully understand itself without taking account of the stream which has flowed forth from it, and in tension with which it has become what it is today."[1]

Leonard Swidler comments: "It is clear that Christianity cannot even begin to know itself except in relationship to Judaism: its founder was a Jew; its sacred Scriptures are Jewish; the first Christians and the first leaders of Christianity were Jewish; its first self-understanding, its first theology, was that of a particular kind of Judaism. It is, however, perhaps less often realized that Judaism too was significantly shaped by its contact with Christianity. For example, the prominence in American Judaism of the feast of Hanukkah is clearly a response to the Christian Christmas; in many ways Reform Judaism was modeled after denominational Christianity. Perhaps one of the most profound ways Judaism was influenced by Christianity was Judaism's shift from being a vigorously universalistic, proselytizing religion at the beginning of the Common Era (when as many as one in ten in the Roman Empire were Jewish, and the numbers were increasing) to being a strongly particularistic, non-proselytizing religion—because of Christian political power."[2]

And third, Karl Barth, in his 1966 *Ecumenical Testament,* stated his conviction that: "We do not wish to forget that there is ultimately only one really central ecumenical question: This is our relationship to Judaism."

Christians, dialoguing with Jews, do so not as Methodists or Presbyterians or Roman Catholics, but primarily as Christians. An immediate benefit of Jewish-Christian dialogue, for the Christian, is thus its ability to draw Christians together.

To the question, Why Dialogue?, there are at least three responses: 1) It helps in the clarification of God's will for humankind. 2) It enables Christianity and Judaism to deepen their own self-understanding. 3) For Christians, it gives us a point of coalescence.

Obstacles to Dialogue

First, the role of Jesus.

In a syndicated column, Alexander M. Schindler, president of the Union of American Hebrew Congregations, reflects on Jewish and Catholic dialogue. He affirms the decision of the recently concluded synod of Catholic bishops not to halt the progress made during the Second Vatican Council. Then he says:

> "On the Jewish side, disappointment has been expressed that the Vatican has failed to establish diplomatic relations with Israel, whose security is a central issue for Jews everywhere. . . . Catholics have grievances, too. Many are offended that Jews do not sufficiently support them on the issue of abortion. . . . Beyond these contemporary issues, there is a more fundamental difference that cannot be resolved and that provides a theoretical limit to our dialogue: the role of Jesus. He is, of course, the predominant figure in Christian religious thought: the son of God, the savior and messiah through whom a 'new' revelation has been brought to humankind, replacing the 'old' revelation on Sinai.
>
> Because this is so, Christianity assigns Judaism only an antecedent role and not a role of full religious equality. It respects Judaism as part of the religious history of Christianity, but it does not and cannot define the Christ event in terms other than that of Jewish displacement. Jewish theology does not give Jesus any role. It sees Jesus, if at all, only as a teacher, one of many such teachers."[3]

Second, the conflict between church and synagogue in the first century.

It has been observed that sometime after the destruction of the Temple in the year 70, the Jewish Christians left the synagogue altogether. Their memory of the events leading to the final break, as preserved in the Gospel of John, make it clear that they felt the synagogue had forcibly expelled them. These events were part of a complex process of "de-Judaizing."

In fact, however, the real and tragic de-Judaizing of Christianity began as a result of the non-Hebraic heritage and anti-Jewish prejudices that many Gentiles brought into the church from pagan backgrounds. Gentile Christians, in defining themselves and the church, did so favorably, and the Jews and the synagogue unfavorably. They defined themselves in terms of being over against.

Third, the role of Christian theology in the emergence of anti-Semitism.

Christians found the biblical promises, blessings, and benedictions reserved exclusively for themselves. The dire predictions, judgments, and warnings were assigned to the Jews. The heroes, the faithful, the courageous were claimed for the church; the unfaithful, the apostates were regarded as belonging to the synagogue. More broadly, the Jews, who were once Israel, were now not considered to be Israel; the Jews, once the accepted of God, were now seen as rejected. The Jewish Law, once valid, was judged as no longer valid. Once within the pale of salvation, the Jews now stood outside it. By means of this selective thinking, Christians began to define themselves so positively and the Jews so negatively, as to escape the prophetic warnings.

As a result, Christians must confess that the cumulative impact of a centuries-long tradition of negative evaluation, even hostility, toward Judaism and Jews, while not the sole cause of the Holocaust, was a condition that aided Hitler's mobilization of public opinion.

Martin Luther, at the beginning of the Reformation, saw that Jews had been maltreated, and expected that, if they were shown kindliness, they would become Christians. When they did not, he published and circulated anti-Semitic venom, which centuries later was potent enough to be used by the Nazis to persuade Christians to accept anti-Jewish measures.

Fortunately, at long last there is a decisive change.

A meeting was held in Stockholm in July of 1983 between representatives of the Lutheran World Federation and the International Jewish Committee for Interreligious Consultations. The Lutherans present offered this statement: "We Lutherans take our name and much of our understanding of Christianity from Martin Luther. But we cannot accept or condone the violent verbal attacks that the Reformer made against the Jews."[4]

Since I am here as a part of the Christian delegation, let it be said without equivocation:

> On the Christian side, genuine Christian-Jewish dialogue can begin only after a profound act of contrition for what Christian Scriptures and theology contributed to the persecution of the Jews, and after a sincere beginning within the church of theological reconstruction.

I think a sensitizing process is underway. Let me illustrate from my own denomination. In a recent publication going to all United Methodist national leaders, both lay and clergy (*Interpreter,* October 1985), there is an appeal to raise money for the United States Holocaust Memorial Museum. It informs us, as United Methodists, that the Holocaust is not just a "Jewish Issue." We are reminded that a study of the Holocaust is as important for Christians as for Jews. The statement recognized that, although the Holocaust encompassed other persons, Jews were its first and most universal victims. The article acknowledges that the Holocaust culminated centuries of the "teaching of contempt" for Jews that permeated Christian doctrines, institutions and societies. Thus theological reconstruction is a prerequisite to dialogue.

This leads, then, to the question:

How Do We Dialogue?

In a booklet by Dean M. Kelley and Bernhard E. Olson titled: *The Meaning and Purpose of Dialogue,* published by the National Conference of Christians and Jews (date unlisted), they indicate what dialogue is not. It is not a sermon, a monologue by one party. It is not small talk. It is not debate. Nobody wins and nobody loses. Nobody scores points or "proves" anything. It is not accusation and defense. A much more useful mode of expression is confession of one's own shortcomings, rather than insisting that someone else confess. Furthermore, dialogue is not a soft-sell approach to conversion.

Should the Christian try to convert the Jew, or the Jew the Christian? The answer is not yes or no! Rather, the question is meaningless, because a person can do no more than witness. If God uses the words of witness to bring about a change, on either side, that is God's work and not ours. But the intent of dialogue excludes conversion. That is not its purpose. Rabbi Abraham Joshua Heschel said: "The presupposition of dialogue is the recognition of the lasting preciousness of each other's commitment. Proselytizing is a major stumbling block to a relationship in which reciprocity and mutual trust are basic."[5]

Fortunately, many Christian churches today officially recognize the need to abandon all forms of unwarranted proselytism of the Jews. Since faith must be a free act between God and the believer, any activity, even the use of social pressure, or other such subtle, psychological devices, is strictly prohibited.

Progress is being made in this understanding.

The Second Vatican Council radically transformed Church attitudes toward this matter of conversion. Billy Graham, (for Evangelical Christians, Graham is more authoritative than the Pope), confidant to several Presidents, the person the media often seek out when they want an expression of a Protestant point of view, following the World Evangelism Congress in Berlin, said: "God, in His own time and way, will judge all men by the light according to which they live. We must distinguish him who lives by no revelation from one who knows that God is revealed in nature, in the world, and in history. The believing Jew's whole approach to life is testimony to his faithfulness to the God of his fathers. Christians must respect such devotedness to God." In his crusades, Mr. Graham says, he makes no special missionary appeal for Jewish conversion. He adds: "Christians must acknowledge that through our faith in Christ we are grafted on to the Jewish people, and we share with them the blessings of God."[6]

Who Represents Whom?

We come, finally, to the question: "Who represents whom when Judaism and Christianity meet?" To what extent can a given Jewish or Christian spokesperson claim to "represent" Judaism or Christianity? Is it possible for a Methodist to speak for Christianity as a whole, and even make suggestions which could be acceptable to a Roman Catholic or a Baptist?

First, within well defined parameters, I do speak for my denomination and you speak for your group. But note: each religious grouping has standards, doctrines, and traditions to which it turns. I might make a pronouncement as a part of the hierarchy of the United Methodist Church, but the validity of the statement would depend on whether it was consistent with the Articles of Religion, the polity of our denomination as outlined in the Discipline by the General Conference, and the general practice and traditions of the church. My authority to speak for my group depends on my faithfulness to the established standards of my denomination. But I do represent my denomination in a variety of settings.

Second, it is possible for me to speak in a limited way for Christianity.

John Wesley, founder of the Methodist Movement in the 18th century, gave a sermon which he titled: "Catholic Spirit." He said that a Methodist is firmly fixed in his religious beliefs, but his heart is open to all. For a Christian, regardless of denominational loyalty, there are certain givens: the Sovereignty of God, the Uniqueness of Christ, the Authority of Scripture. What we have to say about these will vary from group to group, but they are deemed to be important by all denominations. There is a sense in which one Christian can also speak for all Christians in certain faith categories.

Beyond this, however, most of us speak for ourselves. Some years ago, I was asked to write a book about the doctrinal statement in our Discipline. When it was finished the editors were going to give it the title: *United Methodist Beliefs.* I remonstrated that, given our Protestant way of doing things, that title was not appropriate. We compromised on: *Beliefs of a United Methodist Christian.*

I realize that none of us can escape the responsibility on occasion to represent or try to speak for our religious group. I am occasionally called by the press in Minnesota for a United Methodist or Protestant point of view on some issue before our state. It is also a fact that most of us cannot speak for our constituency. They won't permit us! Even the Roman Catholics, with their hierarchical structures, have problems with this. All the polls indicate that the actual practice of Roman Catholics in this country on such matters as birth control differs little from non-Roman Catholics.

When the Right Reverend Edmond Lee Browning was installed as the Presiding Bishop of the Episcopal Church, he had sharp things to say in his inaugural sermon against nuclear arms, racism and environmental pollution. Smith Hempstone, who was Browning's classmate at the University of the South, greeted the elevation of his old friend with an open letter. It's typical of what many in the back pews might say. Hempstone ran through all the grievances from two decades of change: the revision of the 1928 Book of Common Prayer, the ordination of women, the embroilment of the Church in the social activism of the 1960s. "Give us back our church," Hempstone wrote, "and you will be remembered as a good shepherd."

This may be dismissed as the nostalgia of an eminent layperson for by-passed forms. But it is more. It is representative of the gap between pulpit and pew. Leaders of the Church feel there is no alternative to making the enemies of mankind its enemies as well. War, racism, oppression and arms races have to be on its agenda. But the pew wants stability. It wants concern for its agenda: drugs, family disintegration, sexual license, loneliness, emotional emptiness. Leaders must mediate between divergent worlds. As those who presume to speak for the Church press forward with their agenda, a growing number of those in the pew respond by saying: "They don't speak for me."

This phenomenon, of course, is not unique to Christianity.

In a journal titled *American Jewish Archives,* the November 1983 issue focuses on *The American Rabbinate: A Centennial View.* Jonathan Sarna writes an introduction. He distinguished between resisters and accommodators. Resisters have always aimed to reinvigorate rabbinic authority, to lead Jews back toward greater observance of traditional Jewish law, and to counter Americanization. Accommodators have sought what he describes as simulation of American religious norms. The tension between prophet and priest underscores the dichotomy between the idealism of rabbis eager to strengthen Judaism and improve the spiritual condition of their flock, and the pragmatic demands of the laity who evaluate rabbis on the basis of how well they perform their various occupation functions. A down-to-earth eagerness for job security and a practical need to keep their congregations happy pulls them toward being accommodators—not prophets. The congregation establishes the agenda, not the leader. It is a refusal on the part of the laity to accord authority to the rabbi, priest, or pastor, to speak for them.

The Role of the Media

There is one more crucial issue: It is the role of the press in deciding who will speak for Christianity or Judaism, and the issues to be addressed.

The feature article in the 17 February 1986 issue of *Time* magazine was titled, *Power, Glory, and Politics!* It was sub-titled, "Right-wing preachers dominate the dial." The Nielsen survey shows that Pat Robertson reaches over sixteen million households every month. Jimmy Swaggart, Robert Schuller, Jim Bakker, Oral Roberts, and Jerry Falwell all reach more than five million households each month. The article says: "Mainline religion nowadays is a minor force in TV." It continues: "To the dismay of more liberal Protestants, not to mention Roman Catholic and Jewish leaders, the people who have seized spiritual control of the tube are unremittingly Evangelical or Fundamentalist. Four of the top stars are part of the Pentecostal movement, which emphasizes the emotive and miraculous aspects of faith. Sunbelt churchianity is ubiquitous, and whenever there is a political tilt to the broadcasts—which is often—it is virtually always to the right."

At the National Religious Broadcasters convention in Washington, February 1986, these, (and I quote,) "powerhouse preachers strutted their stuff. Jimmy Swaggart roared that the Supreme Court is 'an institution damned by God Almighty' for allowing abortions. Jerry Falwell argued that 'theologically, any Christian has to support Israel, simply because Jesus said to'."[7] The point I wish to make is that the media choose those who will speak for Christianity—for Judaism—and also determine the agenda!

Let me illustrate: In the December 27, 1985 issue of the *American Jewish World,* M.J. Rosenberg writes: "The most important thing to understand about the media is that it loves a bizarre story. That is why Meir Kahane's threats make television screens and newspapers far more often than Prime Minister Shimon Peres' calls for peace through compromise."

He continues: "A few months ago, I asked an American journalist if he intended to write about Israel's decent majority every now and then. Or, would he continue the tradition of focusing on the country's lunatics. The reporter agreed that the good people in Israel constituted the majority of the population by far. But, he added: 'They are not where the action is. There is a different Israel, a new Israel, Kahane and his supporters, religious extremists, crazies of every stripe. They are the story today.'

"I asked him how he would cover the United States if he were a foreign journalist. Would he write about the increasingly tolerant majority or would he focus on those who are bent on creating a religiously homogenous, intolerant America?

"He said that he would certainly focus on the latter. 'Those people are organized and they are growing more powerful. Besides, nuts make better copy.'

Mr. Rosenberg then adds: "I couldn't be too angry with the reporter. He was simply speaking the truth. Nor did I want to echo Spiro Agnew and others like him who have consistently attacked the media for reporting on what's wrong with America, rather than what's right with it. Nevertheless, there is something truly peculiar about the media's fixation on all that is ugly about Israel."[8]

The public often assumes that the person who gets the attention of the media speaks for a particular group. When a Jerry Falwell calls a Bishop Tutu a phony, indicating he does not speak for the blacks of South Africa, some of us would have to add that neither does Mr. Falwell speak for American Christianity, simply because he has access to the media. But he has learned to use the media, and they use him because he has access to the President.

Who speaks for whom? We must sadly conclude that, as far as the public is concerned, the media make that determination.

In summary, we acknowledge that dialogue has its pitfalls. It is difficult to know who speaks for whom. But we must, in humility, keep at this task. In 1972, the General Conference of my denomination issued a statement in which we said:

> "A reduction of Jewish or Christian beliefs to a tepid lowest common denominator of hardly distinguishable culture religions is not sought. A new confrontation of our common roots, of our common potential for service to humanity commends itself to us. Thus, it is the desire of the United Methodist Church honestly and persistently to participate in conversations with Jews."

It is my belief that this statement would be echoed by most major Christian groups in this country. The issue is crucial; the task is challenging; the time to be about it is now.

Notes

1. Dean M. Kelley, Bernhard E. Olson, "The Meaning and Purpose of Dialogue," (publ. National Conference of Christians & Jews, no date), p. 20

2. Leonard Swidler, *Journal of Ecumenical Studies,* Vol. 12 (1975), p. 581

3. Alexander M. Schindler, President of the Union of American Hebrew Congregations, Syndicated Column.

4. J. Halperin and A. Sovik (eds.), *Luther, Lutheranism and the Jews,* (Geneva, 1984), p. 9

5. Kelley, Olson, p. 13

6. Billy Graham, *A.D.L. Bulletin,* (December 1977).

7. "Power, Glory, and Politics!", *Time Magazine,* (17 February 1986)

8. M. J. Rosenberg, *American Jewish World,* (27 December 1985)

Contributors

JACOB B. AGUS (of blessed memory) was Late Rabbi Emeritus, Beth El Congregation, Baltimore, MD and Professor Emeritus of Modern Jewish Thought, Dropsie College, Lower Merion, Pennsylvania.

GEORGE W. BUCHANAN is Professor of New Testament, Wesley Theological Seminary, Washington, D.C.

EMERSON S. COLAW is Bishop, United Methodist Church, Minnesota Area, Minneapolis, Minnesota.

MICHAEL J. COOK is Professor of Intertestamental and Early Christian Literatures, Hebrew Union College—Jewish Institute of Religion, Cincinnati, Ohio

MARTIN CUNZ is Pastor, Stiftung für Kirche und Judentum, Zürich, Switzerland and Editor of *Judaica.*

ALFRED GOTTSCHALK is President of Hebrew Union College—Jewish Institute of Religion as well as Professor of Bible and Jewish Religious Thought.

RONALD M. HALS is Professor of Old Testament at Trinity Lutheran Seminary, Columbus, Ohio.

JAKOB J. PETUCHOWSKI is the Sol and Arlene Bronstein Professor of Judaeo-Christian Studies and Research Professor of Jewish Theology and Liturgy at Hebrew Union College—Jewish Institute of Religion, Cincinnati, Ohio.

RICHARD S. SARASON is Associate Professor of Rabbinic Literature and Thought at Hebrew Union College—Jewish Institute of Religion, Cincinnati, Ohio.

MICHAEL A. SIGNER is Professor of Jewish History, Hebrew Union College—Jewish Institute of Religion, Los Angeles, California.

CLEMENS THOMA is Professor of Bible and Judaic Studies, Theologische

Fakultät and Director of Institut für jüdisch-christliche Forschung, Lucerne, Switzerland.

GEOFFREY WIGODER is Director of the Oral History Division at the Institute of Contemporary Jewry, Hebrew University, Jerusalem, Israel, as well as Vice-Chairman, Israel Interfaith Association. He also serves as Editor-in-Chief of the *Encyclopaedia Judaica*.

Index